# MORE SALES THAN YOU CAN HANDLE

BY ADRIAN FLEMING

More Sales Than You Can Handle

Adrian Fleming
[publisher/imprint]

For information on reproduction please contact
Adrian Fleming,
Charter Gate,
Moulton Park,
Northampton, NN3 6QB,
United Kingdom

reproduction@moresalesthanyoucanhandle.com

First published 2015

ISBN: 978-0-9929185-3-8
(Printed)

ISBN: 978-0-9929185-4-5
(eBook)

To my parents, David and Elizabeth,
my partner Alison, and Jimmy (our dog):
thank you for the years of support,
and the things you have taught me.

Without you all, not only would I have been
unable to write this book, but also I would not
have had the personality, determination and
work ethic I make use of every single day
but I guess that's what makes me who
I am and that's why I do what I do.

# Notes To Readers

It is impossible to guarantee results as Adrian Fleming is not working directly with you and can not see, experience, react to, influence and advise on specific market, product or service factors that will have an impact on results.

The book and all associated materials are only provided on the clear understanding that Adrian Fleming and any other associated party is NOT providing legal, financial, accounting or professional services and advice. People reading and using the information in this book should consult the relevant professionals and service providers before applying what they learn from the book.

This book and associated materials are based on the experience of Adrian Fleming, and as such is intended to provide ideas, strategies, concepts, frameworks and examples that have been used, developed and learned over time and as such are intended to be beneficial to those people who are, or are striving to be successful in sales and marketing, however there can be no guarantee of results and the information may not be suitable or applicable to everybody, as such the information in this book is not guaranteed or warranted to produce any specific results.

At no point is any warranty made in respect to the accuracy and completeness of details and information, even though all reasonable attempts have bee made to verify information provided, as things change over time. Adrian Fleming and all other parties associated with this book respect third party copyright at all times.

Adrian Fleming and all associated parties disclaim any responsibility or liability, loss, risk and damage on a personal or business level as a direct or indirect result of any information in this book and associated material and remind you the use of the information is at the sole discretion of the reader / listener and you should, at all times, adhere to all applicable rules, regulations and laws relevant in the markets in which you operate.

# Contents

# CHAPTER 1

## MAKING POSITIVE THINGS HAPPEN

Welcome. I'm really pleased you're here, because it means you and I have a connection; we both take responsibility for our own future and have a proactive approach to creating a better life for ourselves, and those around us.

The book's title really does describe what's possible for those that take what they learn here and apply it. Even though I'm not there with you and can't guarantee your specific results, what I can say is that just by reading this book, you'll be in a position to potentially shortcut your own journey to success and profit from over 22 years worth of my hard work, investment, real life experiences across many markets and continued quest to build the perfect, replicable and scalable sales and marketing solution.

My vision is for you to be in a position whereby you can generate profitable sales at will, almost as if you are turning on a tap. I make this possible by sharing actionable information in each chapter, with a logic and structure that doesn't just tell you what to do to get sales, it also explains why: ultimately getting as close as possible, in this format, to me working with you on a one-to-one basis.

You see, I didn't create this book to be a literary masterpiece; I created it to help people like you get from where they are now to where they want to be, in the shortest possible time, with the least cost and effort. That's why I've tried to make it as much like a one-to-one conversation as I can, sharing experiences as well as information in a relaxed but informative way.

Another thing I've done in order to speed up and maximise your results is to create tasks for you. So rather than just explaining what to do here in the book, I've produced some free multi-media support materials on a website for you. These are things like: checklists, videos and even specific online training that will allow you to 'go deeper' and get even greater value from this book. All you need to do is go to www.MoreSalesThanYouCanHandle.com to create your account and access all these resources, 100% free.

And just so you know, as we go through the book together, I'll reference resources on the website so make sure that you get yourself signed up quickly!

Now, even though this book is full of proven real-world strategies and tactics that you can profit from right now, I have a word of warning...

...don't try and implement everything on day one: you'll get overwhelmed.

Which leads me on to one of the most common questions I am asked: "What should I do to make money?" Believe it or not the answer is quite straight forward, just the way I like things, no matter what market you work in. So here it is:

• Observe what's required to add value to the market.

• Learn what you don't already know in order to deliver that value.

• Apply what you've learned and get third party help where necessary.

• Sell profitably to the market.

• Repeat the process.

It really is as simple as that. But if you do nothing, which is a risk if you get overwhelmed, nothing will change for you; which is why I gave you that warning. So without further ado, let's get started because taking action is what counts.

I want to share a bit about me and explain what I call ESTO. It's a success principle that I developed and I want to share with you why this makes things really profitable. Turnover and sales without significant profit is what busy fools do. Way too many people, especially in business and sales and marketing, seem to chase sales and turnover as opposed to profit. I've seen it with the majority of salespeople I've observed and many so-called experts and gurus and that's not what I want for you. I want you to be incredibly successful, which means making money.

What are you going to learn and what can you achieve by going through this book?

What you're about to learn is the ability to literally sell anything in any market, whether it's a good product or service or not. The first thing I want to make sure you understand is that I only want you to use what you're going to learn here for good, ethical things – not rubbish, not things that are detrimental to people and societies. You'll find more about these issues as we progress.

The reality is, what I'm going to teach you and what I'm going to share with you, works in every situation. I'm also going to share masses of information, and there's no way you will ever be able to take all this in and apply it all at once. It's actually over 22 years of practical real-life experience, so feel free to go through the book again and again and again. Stop after each chapter or even a small section and just think about what's relevant and how you can apply it.

My goal is to make you extremely successful. What I have here will do that for you, but the reality is even though I'm here helping you through this book, making it happen is all up to you. I can't guarantee your success: only you can.

Let's kick off by just saying that profitable sales can solve virtually any issue. In fact, my father often said, "Throw some money at it," and he was absolutely right. If you're struggling in any area of life, personal or business, if you have profits rolling in on a predictable basis, you can pretty much solve any problem, or at least alleviate it to some extent. The key thing to make sure you understand here is that making money is a good thing.

The other things you're going to learn here, if you really embrace them, mean you can elevate yourself to be in the top 1% of not just successful sales and marketing people, but people in business and in society too. Research suggests that about 1% of people are termed successful. That means they have plenty of money and also plenty of time to make the most of that money. They get to do things, they have the money to do them, and they have a great time.

Only 4% – believe it or not – are doing okay financially and are independent. This is in Western society, so not only the U.K. It's equally true in places like the U.S., Canada, Australia, and similar parts of the world. Only 4% of people are what you would term financially independent.

The rest, 95% of people, are what you would call uncomfortable or, worse still, struggling or broke. I don't want you to be in the 95%. I don't want you to be in the 4%. I want you to be in the 1%. In fact, I want you to go even further than that. No matter whether you own your own business or work for somebody else, generating profitable sales is the simple solution to moving yourself out of the 99% and into that 1% where you are successful.

Believe it or not, anybody can do it. It doesn't matter how old you are, what experience you've had or anything else. You can do this. It's all in your mind-set and we'll go through that later on. I'm here to help you make that happen for yourself.

Now, here's an admission: I'm not a salesperson. I never have been and actually, I never will be in the traditional sense. I'm far too entrepreneurial for that. I can use my time, my effort, my resources and my expertise more effectively for others by helping them and myself at the same time. However, there are other sides to me that you're going to find out about, sides which show why I've been very successful in every single sales environment I have been in, outperforming the sales people every single time.

Sales and marketing success is not actually a result of how hard you work. It's not about how many hours you work. It's about how smart you are when you work. I quite often hear people either in passing or who I work with say to me: "I don't have enough hours in the day," or "I just can't work any harder. I'm doing all I can right now." Those statements are blatant signs that people need to change how they work.

I'm not going to suggest for one minute how to work, how long to work, or how hard you need to work; I'm going to show you the best ways to work and then you can decide from there how you take that forward. You may find working just a few hours a week will deliver all the financial rewards you want; alternatively you may want to keep pushing for even greater profits: it's your decision.

It's not about trading time for money. Success is about maximising value for the market that you're serving and the market you're selling into and having a great enough demand to meet your own personal goals – nobody else's.

There's no shame in recognising that you're in a situation that you're not that happy with at the moment and, maybe, that you don't really know what to do to change things. But the fact is you've invested in this book. Just so you know, I've been there and I've done that too, so I can give you practical help. I'm here to help get you from where you are today to where you want to be.

So, a little bit more about me, as this will help set the scene. I've been in marketing and entrepreneurship for over 22 years now. I've lived and worked in the U.S. and I currently live in the U.K. I was born here, too. Through entrepreneurship, I've had to learn all sorts of skills and one of the biggest skills is salesmanship in a traditional sense, but I don't treat it like that, as you'll find out later.

Here's the other thing. I've always outsold the salespeople I've worked with and employed, even when they've been paid over £100,000 a year. I'm not alone in that because other people who are entrepreneurial and have their own businesses or get involved in other businesses with other people do that, too. An example, in fact, is my partner, Alison. Even though she's not in sales, she has outsold salespeople, too. One particular example was a tradeshow where she was on a stand for a business that I owned, just helping me out. The short story is that Alison outsold all of the experienced salespeople on that tradeshow stand, selling advertising in a magazine, on a subject she knew little about, without a problem. Alison's success added to my enthusiasm and my desire to understand why she and I were able to outsell people who were supposedly 'the best' at sales.

It wasn't just people from one market, industry or environment either who Alison and I could outsell. I've employed people who were originally selling media – advertising space on TV, on radio, in magazines and publications – who were selling marketing services, who worked in telesales or call centres, who sold print. I've even employed people who were selling really high-end brands – like Ferrari and Maserati cars – who were selling office equipment for international brands, selling mobile telecoms and even those who worked in retail stores. There is not one of those groups or anybody who I've employed in any of my businesses, which I'll talk about later, who I haven't outsold.

I've seen what happens. I've also seen superstars in sales 'lose it' and I wanted to know why this had happened and what I could do to resolve it. And that's what this book is going to show you too.

The thing that's come across here, and as we go through this you'll find more and more out about it, is anybody can sell. The sales superstars don't 'lose it', they have a reaction to outside factors; they're the same person and they can still be fantastic salespeople, but they need to have to certain things in place in order to do it; that's what you're going to learn here.

When I work with clients, as well as in my own businesses, I can sell both their products and them really, really well, whether it's products or services, at any sort of value; it's actually what any good salesperson and anybody who's passionate can do.

I've even done it on trade show stands where I've been with a customer and they've been busy, so I just helped out and I've sold for them. I've sold all sorts of things that really I never thought I'd sell, but I understand what you need to do and in what order and I understand the sales proposition – and that's key.

I've had, over the years, business interests across all sorts of things at high and low price points and I've sold both products and services. So at one end of the spectrum, I could be talking about property that's costing hundreds of thousands of pounds, all the way down at the other end to things like stationery, which cost less than ten pence; so it's a really big scale. I've sold in business-to-consumer and business-to-business environments.

I've sold in the U.K. and internationally, too. Not only that, I've sold in person, face-to-face, in meetings. I've sold at a distance over the phone. I've created and designed online resources that sell without the intervention of a human being, for each the mechanics are almost always the same; they follow the same rules. The media in which you sell may change but the results and the way you achieve the results are exactly the same – when you know how.

The first thing to know is that you get results through good education. I'm not talking about a degree from a place like Harvard, Oxford or Cambridge; it's about learning what to do. I've learned the value of this practical education and how it's not about the formal parts; it's about learning what works, what doesn't and why.

The other thing you need is a good work ethic. It's not about working every single hour; it's about working systematically, methodically, logically and knowing what happens when you do something. One of the things I've always found, particularly in my own businesses where I put my time, money and effort into them, is that I've had to solve problems; but I'll tell you what: when your money's at risk, you are incredibly driven – and I am incredibly driven.

Yes, in many cases, I was the brains behind the whole thing, but what I was doing was, for example, selling £60,000 plus deals for a marketing business that I had. Whereas my salespeople, who were very experienced people, who were all telling me they were the best in the business and they were earning six figures, were doing deals at £5000, £10,000 or at most, £32,000. You see, when it came down to it, the actual prospects they were dealing with, when they ended up meeting me or talking to me, wanted to deal with me, not the salespeople, and you'll find out why later on.

Not only that, my salespeople, who I was paying, were saying: "Will you come to the meeting with me?" I was chasing them all the time. That was a mistake. I needed to learn to solve that problem. There's no point in me owning a business and paying people substantial sums of money to chase around after them. That was my biggest mistake, and I took it on board that if I employ somebody or I work with somebody in a sales or marketing or business context, and they're not getting the results that I want them to get, the mistake is mine, not theirs.

Next, I want to share my experiences from over 20 years ago, as they will help you understand why I've been able to sell, even though I'm not a sales person. At the age of 20 I was fortune enough to move to the U.S. and work for a Fortune 500 company. Even though I had some experience before that, which I'll talk about later, this was an incredible learning ground because the first thing that the Fortune 500 company did for me was put me in a completely different selling environment and market than I was used to.

Without going into all the details, within a couple of days of me arriving there, they sent me to the biggest tradeshow and put me on their exhibition stand. Then in the evenings after the exhibition, I attended the corporate social events where customers and prospects were invited to relax and not only talk with people from the company, but meet with major celebrities too. This meant I had to interact with people I didn't know, I had to get to know quickly what that Fortune 500 company really could do for their customers, how they did it and communicate that with complete strangers in a less sales orientated way. This 'baptism of fire' in corporate America ultimately gave me a chance to meet and work with some fantastic people and taught me the value learning fast and those things still make me money today.

I also got to go with the top salespeople for the Fortune 500 company to sales calls, do in-store checks of products and displays, competitive research and consumer research I was sent literally all around the U.S. and into Canada, too, to places as far away as Yakima and Spokane in Washington sate, almost on the Canadian border, or to places like Toronto and Chicago, not just where I happen to be based, which was in Connecticut, to learn why different customers and end users in different states needed different things. I got to see what worked and why their top salespeople were their top salespeople. It was an incredible education and one I'm truly grateful for.

But when I started developing my own businesses and working for myself, investing in other people's businesses, being entrepreneurial and I found that I was outselling other people, I needed to learn what to do. I needed to understand why I could outsell people. I needed to understand what I could do to make my salespeople, my marketing people and my customer service people more effective and to make more money, ultimately for me but also for themselves in the process.

I went out and I completely immersed myself in all sorts of sales systems and strategies. I did things like Jay Abraham's 'Protégé' course. I did things like Tony Robbins' and Chet Holmes' 'Ultimate Business Mastery System'. I've done things like Jordan Belfort's - better known as the Wolf of Wall Street – 'Straight Line Selling System'.

I've read all sorts of books, things like Neil Rackham's 'Spin Selling'. I've done courses with people like Kevin Rogers, who is a comedian-turned-copywriter. I've gone through courses on neuro-linguistic programming, often called NLP, with people like Kenrick Cleveland. I've also studied and done courses with copywriting gurus, because copy is a key component to sales and because when you know what to say, whether it's in person, on the phone, in a video or in writing, you can really turn people on to what you do.

I've learned from and worked with some great people like the late Gary Halbert or the person who's probably the best known or maybe even best copywriter alive today, John Carlton, to really try and refine what I do and how I do it, so as to get predictable, consistent results that I can get other people to accomplish too. When you add this to my entrepreneurial marketing background, too, this becomes incredibly powerful.

The thing is, sales is not just about selling to people for money; it's about persuasion. There are some fantastic persuaders out there: Oprah Winfrey, the late Steve Jobs, Richard Branson, well-known politicians, they're all great persuaders and great salespeople, whether you agree with what they're selling or not. You can learn from those people, too.

The other thing is I am (and those I mentioned a moment ago are) incredibly persistent in their drive for profitability. Most salespeople give up after one or two attempts. They don't have a range of tactics and angles to use. In fact, they're pretty blunt instruments, as I would call them. You need to be the opposite of that, and you also need to be persistent without being a pest.

To give you an example; there's somebody here in the U.K. - I won't mention their name because that wouldn't be fair - but they are a persistent sales and marketing pest. I was sent something by somebody I know who actually said – I'll remove their name from it – "That idiot [the person] is now calling my home number with an electronic message."

Well, that is not going to get them business. They are not doing a great job; they're being a pest. They're actually closing off opportunities because the person who got this message may well have bought from them, but they pushed it too far. You need to be able to balance that, and that's what I'll show you how to do.

I want you to be doing what you do and are best at and representing; not just things that you approve of but things that deliver or solve problems that you value and your market value too. When you have those things in place, you can be a fantastic salesperson and actually get more sales than you can handle, which is a fantastic position to be in because then you pick and choose what you want to do and when you want to do it, and that's a key.

I talked earlier about my ESTO system and I now want to explain this to you. I want to show you and get you to understand and apply this, because once you take what you've learned and use the ESTO system, not only will you be in the top 1% of people out there, where you have plenty of money and time to enjoy it, but you can actually shift into what I think is probably the 0.1% of the most profitable and agile sales, marketing and entrepreneurial people.

One of the people from whom I use many of my figures is Chet Holmes, who was an incredible salesperson; sadly he's longer with us. Chet saw it this way: about 0.8% of people are what he terms 'big-thinking' strategic people. About 99% of people are working tactically and operationally, and I'll explain what that is in a moment. Then you get about 0.1% of people who are actually operating strategically and tactically at the same time. These people normally get the best results.

However, when you put all these things together and you understand my principle, the ESTO principle, you shift into an even better, more profitable segment; the top 0.1% of everybody. That's where you really need to be and will want to be too.

Let me go through ESTO and talk you through it so you can understand the principles behind it.

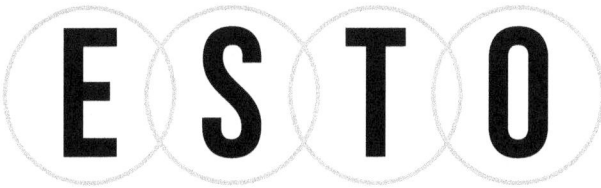

# E S T O

The E stands for Entrepreneurship. Now, I define entrepreneurship as not just starting your own business or anything else like that; I talk about moving the game on, bringing new ideas into the market that you serve. It needs to be an innovation, not just a business.

I need people who are entrepreneurs to be creating new profit, new success and new opportunities in a sales and marketing area. They are looking to identify and develop ideas and ultimately the foundation of a new opportunity that that market hasn't seen yet.

Being in business is one thing – because being in business, you can do things that other people do, too – but the reality is you also need to develop. You need to move the game on, and that is a core factor.

Next is Strategy. Now, strategy is what I would call scalable, integrated thinking; actually making things work. It's all about high-level planning based on specific goals, and we'll talk about goals later. Where there's a degree of uncertainty, you need a strategy. You need to be making it work.

Next is the T of ESTO, and there are three T's actually: Tactics, Techniques and Tools. The three T's are deployable and measurable methodologies. With the tactics, techniques and tools, you're using things and managing things; you're tweaking and monitoring things to see what's working. You're taking specific and specified, isolated events, actions, and activities where specific objectives are the desired outcome. In a physical sense or in digital areas, it enables you to operate and deliver on tactics and improve your efficiency.

Fourth is the O, and that's Operations, the nuts and bolts of making it happen, the doing the work: doing things. In sales, that's a bit different. It could be picking the phone up, it could be arranging to send direct mail out, it could be managing customers and we'll go through all that in much more detail.

As I said earlier, I don't see myself as a traditional salesperson. I don't have the mind-set for that. I work primarily in the Entrepreneurship and Strategy areas, moving slightly into the Tactics, Techniques and Tools segment.

You'll see from the diagram here of the ESTO system, the Entrepreneurship and the Strategy slightly overlap, the Strategy and Tactics, Techniques and Tools slightly overlap and the Tactics, Techniques and Tools and the Operations slightly overlap. That's key, because each of those things influence each other.

Let's talk about the S and T's as two parts because I don't want to get too involved in Entrepreneurship and moving the game on. That's a different subject and may not be relevant for you. I want you to really make things happen based on where you are now, not trying to invent new things; for the moment at least.

When it comes to sales, a strategy is about long-range goals, it's about your market position and it's about how prospects, clients, customers and people like and perceive what you do. That is strategic. Tactics are things such as face-to-face sales, telesales, online selling, advertising, PR, catalogues and brochures; things like that. They're specific things that you can deploy. You can understand how the strategy influences the tactics and you need to learn and know what's happening tactically to modify your strategy to achieve those long-range goals and that market position.

Here's the thing.  It's all very well getting carried away, but if I was working with you  –  and this is really why I've removed the E, the entrepreneurship, from the ESTO principle at the moment – my first job would be to optimise what you're doing right now.  The reason I would do that with you is that once I get that right, I can make you make an awful lot more money and be much more efficient; that way, when we scale up, not only is it self-funding because of the profitability and the money you're making, but you know that the things in place actually already work - there's very little trial and error.

You don't want to be using a trial-and-error approach across multiple things at one time.  If you take it on the ESTO principle, you want to focus time and effort into each of those separately, so you know that when your T's are right and you change something in the strategy, that things should work without any problem.

In your operations, you know that if your tactics, techniques and tools are right, then the nuts and bolts are making it happen.  For example, if a salesperson who goes out and sells face-to-face is not getting the results that your other salespeople are, you know it's him and not the tactics, techniques and tools that he has that's are problem.  It makes it very easy to deal with problems the moment you spot them.

Now, let's just move slightly on from this and say business nowadays is not about products and service; it's about value – creating it, monetising it, and then delivering it and living by it.  That's what I want you to do.

Believe it or not, that's what probably 95% of other businesses either don't do or, worse still, don't have a clear view of their own mind; let alone communicating those values to other people.  And because only 5% of the people out there selling in a marketplace - maybe a marketplace you're after - are not working based on values, then that is an incredible opportunity for you, before we get on to other winning strategies, tactics, techniques and tools – that why you can get to that top 0.1% spot so fast.

I tend to see selling in a different way from most.  I see it actually as a process all about integrating with an end user or your customer.  I'm looking at sales as a way to integrate what I call a 'compelled prospect' to start doing business with you.

Therefore, the shift in that technique has to reflect the needs of you and the business. We don't want you to be out there trying to necessarily shift your proposition and business around based on what somebody else wants. We want it to be right in the first place, and we'll go through all that.

Sales are a transition. A transition from somebody being a prospect to being a customer . As I said, my number one job in sales is to perfect that transition part, because it pays for itself. I would be looking at using the ESTO principle, or certainly the strategies, tactics, techniques and tools there to get your cost under control. I would be looking to deal with a specific segment of the market so that I can really focus my attention and your attention on the best and most profitable segment you can and then dominate it.

Too many people in sales, marketing and business have too big a target audience. Did you know, for example, that people like Apple, who are incredibly successful and profitable, or IKEA, again incredibly successful and profitable in a completely different environment, are only targeting somewhere in the region of 5% to 10% of the overall market? They do that because it's a strategic goal. They can then tailor their tactics, techniques and tools for that alone and that's where the profit is.

They leave the rest of the profitability of the market alone, so somewhere between 90% and 95% of other opportunities, which in real terms is probably only about 50% of the profit in the market, to the other people. Successful companies dominate their chosen niche and profit because of that. They reduce their overheads, they reduce their costs, they focus on developing that niche and that's where good entrepreneurship starts to come in.

Those factors are reasons they are the most successful in their markets. Let other people scrabble around and fight each other for the non-profitable or less profitable areas. You need to take that aspect on board. I want you to focus on the most profitable segment of your market; but don't worry; we'll cover how to do that later.

Just to bring things to a close in this chapter, I'll tell you what I do. When I work on my own things or when I work with people as private clients, the first thing I do is try to perfect what they're doing at that particular moment. In doing that, the first part is to help to determine if they can make enough money in a market. Will it actually pay, and how will it pay? How can they maximise it?

There are too many people out there, as I started off by saying, who are working too many hours; working all the hours they can. If they own the business, they're slogging their guts out and sometimes actually paying for the privilege of being busy and there may not be the profit they want in their market - just to add insult to injury.

I'm looking at the whole market and asking is the market right for them? Are they targeting it in the right way? As a guide, are others profiting in the market or in a similar market that you can piggyback off, learn from or things like that? That would be my first port of call.

I want you to go away from this first chapter and start thinking about what you do and who you sell to. I want you to stop trying to sell to everybody, because at the core, it's the best way to profit, and never, ever let the prospect determine the price you sell at because that is a sure-fire way to not be profitable, not make sales and not be successful.

# CHAPTER 2

# THE PRINCIPLES OF FAILURE AND SUCCESS — BOTH ARE POSITIVE

In this Chapter I want to cover the fundamental aspects of sales that I, and the best in the business, live by, so you can model them, modify them and incorporate them into what you do day-to-day. I'll also clear up any confusion, so that you're absolutely clear on the most important elements, before you waste any time, money or effort on the wrong things.

I hope I don't have to say this, but just to be sure I will: you need to hold yourself accountable, because you are the one who is going to make this happen, nobody else. With that in place, first of all, from a 'what to do' point of view, people need to pay attention to what you have and offer and, as a result, engage with you. If they don't, you have absolutely no chance, you're going to fail.

But here's the thing. If you are going to fail, you want to fail fast. The first thing for most people that's really quite counterintuitive, even uncomfortable, is that as you start out on a new sales process, marketing process or an entrepreneurial process – believe it or not – you should try to fail and fail fast. Too many people look for 'green shoots' of hope at first. They look for people to say: "That seems like a good idea," or "That will probably work."

Actually, what you need to be doing is looking for bad news; looking for reasons not to do something as opposed to reasons to do something. This is going to save you vast amounts of time, money and effort, even though it's counterintuitive. It's absolutely critical that you do this even though instinctively you don't want to. You want to succeed, but actually failing, and as Google puts it, 'failing forward and failing fast,' is really positive.

I'm not suggesting you deliberately do things the wrong way, that's just silly. Do what you think is right and see what's not working: who knows you may have a 'hit' on your hands from the outset, but if you do fail, and you analyse what you did, you'll see what to do and what not to do in the future.

I want you to try and fail within an hour or within a day or within a week, depending on what you do. Best of all, I also want you to try and fail with minimal investment in time, money and effort because the more times you fail – believe it or not – the bigger your success will be. I know this is something that most people struggle to get their heads around, but it's absolutely true. It's actually what the most successful businesses out there do.

Google and Facebook are very well known for investing in so many projects that never come to fruition because they're trying to fail. When they only fail on a small scale they can be almost certain they are on to a winner.

Through those failures, you actually come up with highly successful ways of doing things. Even on a basic level, with a marketing idea or a sales technique, or going back to the ESTO principle with the strategies, the tactics, the tools, the operations – all of those things require failure until you perfect them. You want to build something that's almost a machine, a system that you can rely upon, that you can almost turn on and off as and when you want profitable customers.

I've talked about failure, but you want success, understandably; so you need to be looking at a market to enter. Most people, unfortunately, look at a product or a service; and that's a mistake. Another common mistake is when you and your friends think something is a great idea, but the reality is, you are not your customer and in most cases, you and your friends are not able to provide a sustainable, profitable future.

Again, I know this is counterintuitive because if you think it's a great idea and your friends think it's a great idea and you ask a few people and they think it's a great idea too; you think it's a sure-fire thing. But you need to be looking at a market sector and not focusing on a product or service.

In fact, when I deal with people on a one-to-one level, just by changing their product or service after we've done market research, they usually radically shift their results in a positive way. Trying to 'flog a dead horse' is never going to work, but as soon as you get something that's right and the market adopts, the market loves and the market embraces, you are onto a winner.

All highly successful entrepreneurs, marketing people, and salespeople are actually what I would call 'number crunchers' and 'number people' because results and successes is a numbers game; it's not an emotional game at its core, no matter what other people tell you. You always hear people talk about features and benefits and things like that, but let's be clear here: for you to get more sales than you can handle, you need to be focused on numbers, but not in a boring way, as we'll cover.

Whilst we're at it, the other thing is: don't try and create a new market. If others are in a market and doing well, then that's a great target market. I've made this mistake on many occasions – and it's an expensive mistake, too, having invested £10,000s if not £100,000s trying to do this in the past. Something I don't recommend! Unless you have some serious money behind you or you're damn lucky, you're going to struggle to create a new market. Look at markets that are successful, where other people are doing well, and you can do well, too.

You're probably asking: "But if other people are in a market, why should I be in it?" Here's the thing: virtually every market has space for you, if you know how to spot that space. When you focus on what the competition is doing, you will spot the space.

You might be able to 'piggyback' off what somebody else is doing; you might be able to 'piggyback' off a trend. For example, you hear about things like the 'selfie stick'. It's just a stick you put your phone on to allow you to take pictures of yourself from a greater distance. That sort of thing didn't exist very long ago, but there was a market, there was a demand.

You can actually spot what the competition is doing in a market. They may actually not be competition; you may be complementary to them. But as soon as you're aware of what they do and what they do well and probably more importantly, what they don't do or do well, this will actually guide you to success.

Here's the other thing: most people complicate things, particularly when it's their own product or service. Again, they're focused on that product or service. They think that all these features and factors and elements are really, really important. I want you to strip away all the complexity and get back to really being able to communicate and keep things simple and easy to understand, because that's the key that's going to make you highly successful.

It's a really important thing for you to embrace what you do, but more importantly – going back to what I said earlier, you and your friends are not your customers – it's other people who need to clearly see why they should be spending their time, money, and effort with you and keeping things simple will make this process far easier for you.

Next, let's talk about sales. One thing that marketing expert Dean Jackson, who you may or may not have heard of, talks about and clearly states is selling occurs before during and after money changes hands, so you need to be thinking about selling all the time.

As I said, selling is not actually trying to convince somebody to give you money – we'll go far deeper into that later – but selling occurs before somebody gives you money, as they're giving you money and also after you've had their money. Think about those three segments within what you do, and later on, we'll start to perfect that so it's right in your own situation.

Remember, I don't want you to separate out these concepts of sales, marketing and business; I want you to mould them all together because at the end of the day, it is all one thing, and I'll give you a definition in a moment on that. I want you to dispel the traditional view that sales and marketing are different and stop acting in that way. Smart sales and marketing people know that's the case.

Smart sales people also know that they need to run what I call campaigns, which are multiple things, not just one, in order to generate sales, and do this consistency as an overall communications strategy. If you expect specific, single events to generate more sales than you can handle you're going to be disappointed.

Going back to my ESTO framework, we're talking about a strategy, we're talking about using multiple tactics and techniques and tools. Too many people think that sales are events. They're not; they're part of continual process. It's not, 'Do something once and sales will happen.' Again, we'll talk about that in greater detail later on.

People and you also tend to say things like: "I should do this," or "I should have done that." That's not helping you in the goal of making sales. You need to think from a personal point of view and from your prospect's point of view, concentrating on how to change their understanding and language. You might change the way somebody thinks from thinking: "I should do that" to "I must do that."

We're looking not to convince people; we're looking to compel people to take the action you want them to take. I have a few rules in place because compelling something to happen, compelling people to do things that you want them to do, can be quite detrimental if you don't use it in the right way because it's so effective. If you remember, we said at the start, we only want to use all the things you're learning here to make you incredibly successful in a positive way.

First of all the rules is: we're not selling in an environment where we have Maslow's hierarchy of needs at a basic level (I've created this graphic for you that explains it in a little bit more detail).

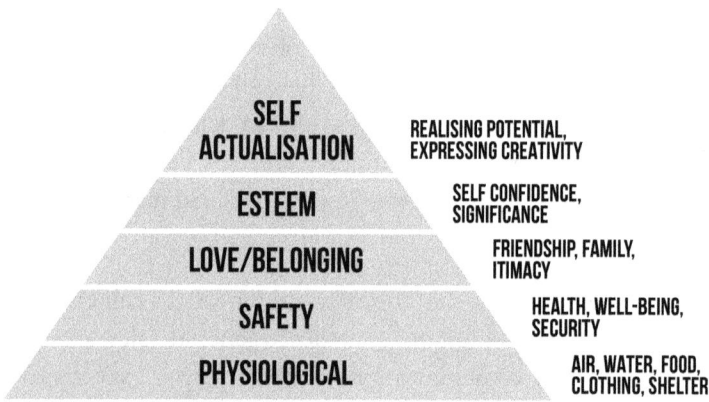

SELF ACTUALISATION — REALISING POTENTIAL, EXPRESSING CREATIVITY

ESTEEM — SELF CONFIDENCE, SIGNIFICANCE

LOVE/BELONGING — FRIENDSHIP, FAMILY, ITIMACY

SAFETY — HEALTH, WELL-BEING, SECURITY

PHYSIOLOGICAL — AIR, WATER, FOOD, CLOTHING, SHELTER

In the Western world, here in the U.K. the U.S. and places like these; people are not in need of the basics of life the way they used to be maybe 50 or 100 years ago. Things have changed.

Most of the time when you're selling, it's a 'nice to have,' not a 'need to have.' You're not likely to be selling people air or food, at least in a sustainable way. You might be selling food or drink in a pleasurable way, but people have sustenance to keep them alive. The health care may not be perfect, but it's fundamentally there. Things are different now, and you need to be aware of this.

You need to make sure that wherever you sell to an audience and whatever you're trying to compel people to do is for the right reasons. On this basis, it's about creating value, and here's the thing: it has to create value for the people who buy but it also has to create value for you, too. There are too many people selling things that are not of value to themselves.

As I said earlier, I want to give you a phrase that helps combine sales and marketing because I want you to put them together. What I'm going to use is a quote from Dan Sullivan, who's the founder of Strategic Coach, which is an excellent program for entrepreneurs who have reached a success of a certain level. Dan has a great definition which I think really sums it up well. He talks about marketing, but sales to me is in the same area, and you'll see why in a moment.

Dan's quote is: "Marketing is any activity that gets people intellectually engaged in a future result that's good for them and getting them to emotionally commit to take action to achieve that result."

There are some components in there that I think are really important. Number one: 'intellectually engaged'. Well, that requires people to have the thoughts. They need to know what they're doing. You don't try to kid people or con people here. You get them intellectually engaged.

Next, you have 'a future result that's good for them'. Again, that's what you should always be doing.

Then the third part I want to draw your attention to is this part of 'emotionally commit', because when people have emotion and they want to take action, the selling part – and this is what a huge number of salespeople don't appreciate or understand – is a formality. At any price, the concept of "closing" a prospect becomes redundant; I'll talk more about this later, but a close should be a natural thing, because the person wants to do something because they want the end result. There need not be any pressure selling at all.

You can now also see that there's nothing wrong with selling and making money if you're doing it in a positive way. Actually, society doesn't work if you don't sell and you don't make money, so don't be afraid to sell or to make money. It's something people struggle with sometimes.

Here's another one: you decide if you sell, not the prospect. Let me give you an example here. One of my businesses is involved in a specific type of cross-media marketing. Without giving the names of people involved away here, because it wouldn't be fair, I was working with a very well known U.K. national newspaper group; they're a very big business to say the least and sell many millions of newspapers a day.

We had an agreement with them and they were going to use our intellectual property and skill and share in the revenues and profitability. It was a true a win-win deal for both parties. However, they didn't exhibit to me – and at the end of the day it was my business and my decision – the characteristics that I felt they should, so I decided not to work with them.

Now, I know some people will think that's daft because it was potentially highly profitable, but I knew that the amount of time, money and effort we had to put into it based on the way they were acting may not actually turn out for the best for us as a business, so I made the decision not to work with them. It was my decision, not the prospect's, even though they wanted to do things.

I encourage you to put yourself into a position, by learning what you have and applying it to what you do, so that you can decide if you want to sell or not. Never think: "I have to sell because…" for example, you need to meet the payroll, pay the bills, keep a job, or anything else. You need to be so good at what you do that you are the one making the decision to sell or not.

That also leads you into an ability to take advantage of opportunities and dismiss things that are not opportunities as and when they present themselves. That's the perfect way to look at what you do, how you do it and move forward in the right way for you and not a third party.

Here's the other thing. You have to put the effort in. There's no such thing as easy money nowadays, it just doesn't happen. Yes, you might get a bit lucky here and there, but I want you through this nook to realise that you need to put effort in. You don't need to work all hours and risk everything, because that's not what it's about, but there has to be effort.

That effort needs to go into building what I call habits and those habits are things you automatically do that convert prospects into customers; this way it will happen naturally, not just for you, but for other people you work with and for your prospects, too.

How do you do this? Habits can be quite negative. People have a habit of smoking, drinking, taking drugs, eating too much food, not doing exercise. There are lots of negative things, as you can see, but there are an awful lot of positive habits too. The great thing is that human brains are actually geared up to make life easy; they are looking for things to adopt as habits. The brain deletes or puts aside, distorts and generalises all the time and that is its way of making sense of things.

Your brain wants to make sense of everything around it, but it's not that easy. There's an awful lot going on, so it deletes things, it distorts things, it generalises things and it makes things up, too. But if you understand that – and as we go through this you'll see how that works – you could start to persuade and to build habits in your prospects.

How best to start that motion? I want you to start looking at a market. When you look for problems in that market that you feel you could actually find and potentially resolve - both internally and externally, for you and for other people – you will find solutions and you will be able to present solutions to your prospects.

One of the best ways for you to do that and to start getting people on your side – and we'll go into this in a lot more detail – is to actually teach. Every time you teach people something that they don't know, you gain. By gaining power in a relationship that differentiates you from any potential competitor and even in the relationship you are building.

Almost all sales people tend to talk about products and services. To counter this, you may have noticed there have been lots of studies, books, ideas and strategies about features versus benefits and things like that, or consultative selling . All these tactics are relevant to a degree, but when you talk about products and services, no matter how you do it, even as a consultant, you're seen in a sales capacity. And have you ever noticed that salespeople tend not to be liked? Just think about when your phone rings in the evening with a telesales call. How many times do you think: "Oh, great, somebody wants to sell something to me?"

So people tend not to like salespeople and don't like to be sold to. However we all love people who help us, we can't not as it's one of our in-built habits. Another positive side-effect is this also builds what's called reciprocity, which is where people feel obliged to do something helpful in return – like buying from you.

Think about it from a personal perspective here. Imagine somebody's trying to sell to you. Do you want somebody to be sitting with you, talking about a subject, who's just a salesperson? Probably not.

What about if they were a consultant? Well, that consultant is probably more knowledgeable, listening to you and responding based on what you say, not just running through a sales pitch, and that is a much more powerful position to be in. Being a consultant is not difficult; you really only need to know more than the person you're sitting with.

But more than that. Here's where the real power and influence comes in to play; you need to be seen by your prospect as an expert or a guru on a particular subject, the subject in which you are presenting a solution to the market. You will be seen as a leader, an authority, an innovator and be able to change a situation for them, which is the key.

I want you to stop thinking as a salesperson and not even really think as a consultant, but I want you to become an expert, a guru, an influence or an authority in your chosen market and I'm going to show you exactly how to do that.

Trust me when I say it's - first of all- not difficult. Second of all, it's much more profitable, because people always pay much more to hire an expert or guru compared with a salesperson or a consultant, so put yourself in that position when you're out there presenting to a marketplace. Most of all, as that expert or guru, you'll find you enjoy the process a lot more because people will open up to you, and that's a key factor.

If you do just that, turn up on time and do what you say you're going to do – which is another thing that I see too many people in sales and marketing not do – you'll be able, without any other changes at all, to improve your sales results by at least 20%. This very simple step has a 20%-plus improvement in your results, and that is amazing before we get into anything else.

Let's talk about a few techniques as you need some tactical things here at this stage that we can develop through the book. Because you're coming at things from a different angle now, you need to get your prospects to make decisions, not try and 'close" them and on that basis saying 'No' to you and your proposition is no problem. It actually gives you a chance to learn and resolve objections, or ultimately walk away in a positive way without forcing the sale.

Too many salespeople keep banging the door in an attempt to make the sale and actually that's not great. Somebody saying no to you actually isn't a problem; there are some real positives to that that we'll cover later.

You've probably heard the phrase, 'People buy from those they know, like and trust.' I'm going to show you how to make this happen incredibly quickly and without fail. We'll cover that later, but here's the thing and I see this all too often: you have to believe in what you're selling. You can sell if you don't believe in your product or service, trust me; I've seen it happen, we all have. Well known people have done it too. If your drive for money is strong enough, it's no problem to sell a product or service that you yourself would not recommend to a friend or family member, but it's a short-term situation and not what a good honest person does.

I've seen too many people, even ones who have worked for me, not really understand or believe in what they're selling. These sales people move on quickly, they don't do the numbers and they're definitely not an asset to any business because they're not an asset to the customer.

You have to believe in what you're selling and you have to understand what you're selling, too, to be that expert or guru to the prospect. Remember, you don't need to be a real expert, just an expert to your prospects. By understanding the market and those who buy into it, you can genuinely help people by being that expert, and that's the goal.

I want every salesperson who works for me or with me to really get into and understand what they're selling. I've seen too many people not take an interest in what they're doing; it's just a job. Jobs are not what people who are successful have, only people who want a job and want to get by.

Selling is a step-by-step process. For example, Jordan Belfort, better known as the Wolf of Wall Street, has what he calls the Straight Line System, and that is a very good way to look at it. I'm going to take it further than that later on, but you do already, on some level, know that taking somebody from being a completely cold prospect to being a customer requires you to follow a path and the quickest way to get them from one place to another is a via a straight line so Jordan is absolutely right and that's why he was so successful in sales, even if it wasn't always ethical or legal.

You have to understand that there are steps along that sales process that you need to cover and we'll cover those later on, but it's important that you know this as a basic technique. You also need to know about cross-selling and up-selling; for example, you see on Amazon where somebody buys a book or you enter in some information and it says: "People who bought this item also bought this." That's an example of cross-selling and up-selling.

In general you should be looking to sell more of things that are good for them. You're looking to upgrade people to a VIP level of service or a more complete solution for their needs, or something like that. This upgrading approach to sales is essential as that's where real profit comes, because the cost of acquiring a new client is really high, so you want to make the most of every one of those clients you have.

Another way to do this is to have an alternative sale. You want to make people happy and it's the right thing to do, but sometimes, people struggle to justify a particular price point that you've set. So a good strategy may be to have a lower-priced option that gives prospect a chance to try something at a lower price and therefore, as price is a factor for many people, lower risk too.

Equally, you may have a more expensive option, because people tend to think that more expensive is better. I know from my perspective, if there's an opportunity to have a better experience, a VIP experience, a more expensive experience, that's the one I want to take because I believe through experience, and probably a level of stupidity just like everybody else, that more expensive is better. You want to have those different price point options in your 'bag of tricks'.

Also, from a sales point of view, because this is also the way people are, you have to be goal-oriented; something we'll look at later. All goals must look at the lifetime value of that customer, not just the one-off sale.

There are some times when you only make one sale, but more and more – and we'll talk about this a little more in detail later – there are multiple opportunities to extract value out of customers. I want you to do that, because getting more sales than you can handle is one thing, but really profiting from them is another.

When you know where the prospect sits, in terms of their existing knowledge on the subject, you can move them along this step-by-step process, this straight line, more logically and therefore easily. I want you to be able to not just answer frequently asked questions, I want you to be able to tell prospects what they don't know and start them on a process where they find out what they need to know and what they don't know they need to know too; this really positions you as the expert and guru.

The other thing is -and I see this all the time with salespeople - is that you have to recognise what I call 'people fishing'. These are people who are trying to find out what you do and how to do it. We'll talk about that a little bit more later on. People actually are really geared up nowadays to not just ask why something happens but how it happens too; it's an automatic instinct we have.

I've seen salespeople over and over again spend time, money and effort going to meetings, talking to people on the phone, helping people out and not making a sale. It's because the people they're investing their time, money and effort with – and my time, money and effort too – are not buyers; they're fishing. You have to recognise these people.

To be really successful you must tap into what's called prospect neuropsychology; this is quite a different idea, but in simple terms you need to target people in a certain way and you need to give them aspirations, aspirations that: (a) they want to buy into, (b) they can afford and (c) they believe they can achieve. This last one is the most powerful, yet the one most sales people ignore or don't appreciate.

The goal or outcome you offer your prospect has to be just above what they think could be achieved; a bit like being just outside their comfort zone. You don't want to be doing things and saying: "Here's a really big idea," or presenting a distant target. You have to set something that somebody really is compelled to buy into, to take action on because they can see it, want it, can afford it and can believe in their ability to get it too.

You also have to be positive. You'll find that people sell not just positive opportunities and good things, but they also sell to avoid pain, which is a really great thing. You have to be positive even if you're selling to avoid a painful situation.

Because you're looking for people to take action, not ask questions – because that's what it's about – you need to be able to use questions to control a situation and use your tonality to control a conversation and guide your prospects. Again, we'll talk about this later.

When you've overcome each component of the process, the straight line that Jordan Belfort talks about, you should be able to move the prospect nearer to a sale; but you have to know what outcome you expect as you move along that line. Without this you will not ultimately make a sale, should that that's the right thing to do.

You need to understand after each engagement – whether it's one where you're present or not, on the phone, in person, at a tradeshow, whatever – what should happen next, because if that's not what's happening, you can and must modify how you act in order to get that outcome.

There is very little variation in the route from somebody being a prospect to being a customer for a specific sales engagement; people think there is but actually there isn't and that's why you need to know what outcome you should expect and if you don't get it, modify things accordingly.

In a sales and marketing scenario you need to be persuasive and that's actually why really good salespeople can sell things that don't even exist yet; they're persuasive and they can manipulate a situation, but not in a negative way, to move people along that line.

Remember, don't be afraid to fail – because you will – and just putting in the effort will get you respect with prospects and if you work for somebody else, with your boss or the owner of the company.

It's not just the results: it's the effort that counts. Be prepared to give up your time and energy for something you really believe in, but know what you're prepared to give up too so that you're not a busy fool; you're not working all hours and not making the money.

So, at this point we've come to the first task.

If you go to the website www.MoreSalesThanYouCanHandle.com, there will be some more information to help you there. I have a few small tasks for you because doing these tasks is going to move you along the line from where you are now to where you want to be.

The first of these is actually on a more personal level. I want you to understand and to analyse where you are now, and be realistic.

How happy are you?

What are your sales?

What really are you not getting, whether it's from your boss or from the way you run things?

Remember when answering these questions you need to know factually, realistically - not in an over or under exaggerated way - where you are now. You then need to identify where you want to get to. This might be financial, it might have to do with the number of hours you work, it might be the way you work.

I want you to know where you are now and where you want to get to, because if you don't know where you want to get to, you're never going to get there.

When I present at conferences and things like that, I quite often use the analogy of a map. There's no point using a map or even your sat-nav in the car if you can't tell it where you want to get to, because you'll never get anywhere meaningful.

So you need to know where you want to get to and from this at least have some ideas of how you're going to get there. Let's bring that back to the ESTO principle I talked about earlier.

Where you are is fairly straightforward.

Where you want to get to is about strategy.

Remember, we talked about how things are not fixed and actually may change over time, but that's great because you know where you want to get to - that's the strategy.

You know where you want to be positioning yourself in a marketplace, how people see you, how people appreciate what you do.

Then you need to move into the tactics and the techniques and the tools, those T-components: those are the basis of how you're going to get there. You don't have to get these components 100% right at the moment, but you need to have an idea of how you're going to get there.

In the next part of the task, I want you to define the market you sell to.

Next, I want you to define your ideal customer.

This could be in what they spend, how they are living, their age, even their name because names are often associated with certain types and groups of people; you'll sometimes hear people call this definition a 'customer avatar'.

I want you to define that perfect person or that business, for what you do, as best you can. What I would say, however, is, if you're selling business-to-business, you're still going to have a person buying from you, so think about the person as well as the customer.

Next, I want you to define your current customers, if you have them already.

Are they your ideal customers? If not, identify the differences.

Lastly as your task here, I want you to understand and to note down what are the three to ten things that people should know before buying what you sell or do?

That way, you can start to build a pitch. These are three to ten things that your ideal prospects may understand or know or they may not. I want you to write those down.

So those are your tasks for this part. Once you've done those, come back, keep going through the book, and we'll travel further along the straight line, from where you are now to where you want to get to.

# CHAPTER 3

# THERE'S NO SUCH THING AS A GOOD SALES PERSON

In this chapter, and from this point on, we're going to set things up so you can make a quantum leap in your results. It's the results you're looking for too, not results that just occur.

The first aspect to appreciate is, in my experience and with those I work with, too; good salespeople don't actually exist. I know that's a pretty bold statement, but they are really good at taking orders. And that's the best news you could have, whether you're a business owner or in sales or marketing, because it's a replicable, teachable skill and results can be scaled. I don't want to be derogatory to people who makes sales and make money doing it; it's just that any business has to make sure it's not reliant on a single person or a small number of people.

If you're making sales and you're good at it, as soon as you can systemise what you do, how you do it and why you do it, your level of success will multiply exponentially. It will work just as it did for someone like Jordan Belfort, even before his Wolf of Wall Street days, when he was a sales sensation, long before he became notorious, famous or whatever what you want to call it.

Here's the other thing. Sales people and companies would rather take orders, because it's less stressful, it's easier and it's a much lower cost. So, when you have this strategy in place, it's an incredible win for everybody involved. Why would you want to make life harder than it needs to be?

Let me explain to you what will make the perfect order-taker as a person. The first thing is that people seem to think that good salespeople are what you might call bubbly, extrovert people; these type of people are what I would call good cold callers. They have what you call a thick skin. They don't mind people saying no to them. But that doesn't necessarily make them good sales people.

Actually, I've had many people work for me, or I've worked with teams of people, who have lots of these extrovert personalities and they don't necessarily make good salespeople. They don't convert prospects in to customers all that well most of the time. If you have these people - maybe you're one of them - look at that dynamic and assess the role that they are best suited for. They are an asset when working in their natural way, but expecting them to be the best at sales could be a mistake.

Next, being busy is not the same as being productive. The two are very different, as you'll soon come to appreciate. You have to do what works, not what's comfortable or fun to do. You're not in business to have fun; you're in business to make money; though if you can have fun along the way, that's a bonus!

As a great salesperson, you have to balance your empathy with your ego. Salespeople tend to have quite a big ego if they're good. It's no bad thing, but you have to balance that because too big an ego with not enough empathy will not go down well with customers, clients or prospects.

You also have to balance your excitement and determination with your planning ability. Planning is where success comes from; it's not just about excitement and determination. That's because no matter what people say, good salespeople are not born, they're developed, they're learning all the time, they're replicable.

People who are good in sales are actually very much disciplined people and they take action. Not only that, they become an asset to their customers or clients. Here's the thing. People don't tend to abuse their assets, they value them. What will happen when you become an asset to your prospects is you'll need to work less to gain and retain their loyalty and trust whilst at the same time win their business. On top of this, your customers and prospects will almost certainly and instinctively protect you, because people, believe it or not, will work harder to protect what assets they already have than they will to acquire new ones. That's something that we'll come on to later.

In terms of sales, as I say, it's all about results; but results are not the same as sales. It's about the impact of a good salesperson on the business. Too many salespeople are actually not great for your business. I often see situations where people who make the sales are causing all sorts of problems within their organisation, leaving other people to pick up the pieces behind them.

So for you to be a great salesperson, or have great sales people work for you, make sure the impact on the business is a positive one and not one where sales activities cause chaos for others and leave a trail of destruction behind that other people have to sort out.

Also, becoming a good salesperson is about being coachable. Good sales people are hungry for success and use education to their advantage, appreciating what needs to be done and applying that to feed their hunger.

As we said earlier, we want to instil in all salespeople the values of the business. If it's your business, it's your values; if you work for somebody else, it's their values. When you understand the values behind the business, you can really perform at a much higher level much more easily. That way, it also encapsulates the fact that selling is not all about the close either. Too many salespeople are confused by trying to get the closing technique right. As I've said, it's a natural thing to happen. Sales is not all about the close.

Salespeople must, for the sake of themselves, their business, prospects, clients and customers, see things as they are, not see them better or worse than they are. Doing this can be used as a sales and marketing technique and later on we'll talk about how to help the client move forward along that line and those points necessary to make a sale, that take people from being a prospect to a customer, all through being factual.

Generally in sales, you want to have what I call a 'Perfect Sales Attitude'. You need to manage your time really well. You need to think strategically, not just tactically. You have to have great communication skills, not just with prospects, but also with other people you work with: your colleagues, your associates, your suppliers. Great sales are all about things like your follow-up and your presentation skills.

Be honest with yourself, and with your prospects. If you are and you are not going to do things that actually are detrimental – for example, saying things to your colleagues behind a prospect's back that you wouldn't say to them directly - you'll find that those values, those skills and those abilities will become truly valued by anybody you work with, not just somebody you're trying to sell to.

I've seen way too many people work for a company that has a specific brand ethos that just don't operate in that way. Great companies who are successful don't allow this to happen, which is why the staff in an Apple store are well trained, passionate about what they do and the brand they represent, and to me, do a great job.

On the opposite end of the spectrum, here in the UK, another electrical retailer had a survey for customers as they left the store. The survey was very simple and asked for customers to press a green or red button at the exit to say if the service they had was good or not good. It was quite a fun and effective way to survey the customers I thought. But in reality the staff at this store seemed far less customer orientated than those working for Apple. This was demonstrated by the fact that, when buying something there, I was told by the person working on the cash desk, after I had waited a few minutes to be served, to press the green button as I left the store. There was no mention of why, no real customer service and no passion for the place of work, just concern about getting a good review.

Another example of this - I won't name names again - but it's a very well known U.S. magazine in the business sector that prides itself on how they really support people and entrepreneurship. When I had dealings with them they were anything but that within their own organisation. People there just had a job. They didn't actually live the values of the actual publication, and that was wrong, that's why they're going to be limited in their success, which is a shame.

Here's another thing. You need to be able to say no and be okay with that, because you'll find that your best results come from actually saying no and having what I would call a 'not-to-do' list, because 'not-to-do' lists are far more beneficial to you and your business than a 'to-do' list and they're far more profit-oriented.

It's okay, as well, not to respond to people in a fashion that doesn't suit you. For example, even in sales, you don't want to be so accessible that you're not productive. As I said earlier, being busy is very different from being productive.

People send e-mails all the time and one of my pet hates is people who send an e-mail and if they don't hear back in the next two or three minutes phone me up. E-mail and phone calls are there to drive somebody else's timeframe. If you control your e-mail, you control the communication; you control what you do and when you do it. Your productivity will massively increase. In sales, that will lead to greater sales. So don't feel obliged to do things, especially if they're not a perfect fit for what you do and how you best manage your time.

I also want you to know that I will actually fire clients too, and I encourage you as a great salesperson to do the same. You don't want to waste your time and their money, taking on the wrong customers.

The other aspect I want to cover here – I'll take it from my own perspective – is that I only work with people I want to work with. In my case, I only want to work with entrepreneurial people and businesses that are coachable. You need to know who you should work with and want to work with because when you do that, you will add more value to that person, work better with them and have a better rapport; and sales is almost always about rapport.

To be successful in sales you also need to make sure that what you sell to them works. When you actually sell something that you know works, that's when you actually get the real results. You should think to yourself: 'Would I actually sell this item if I only get paid when my customer gets the end result I promised?' If you can hand-on-heart say yes to that, then you're in a great place and you're selling exactly what you should be selling. You'll also know that what you're selling is compelling, so you don't actually need to convince somebody, and that is the right way to operate.

The only reason to give up what you're doing, when marketing or selling something, is when it's either no longer fun or meaningful. Fundamentally, you should never give up because giving up is not a way to make sales. When it's fun and you know that what you provide is meaningful, it gets the results and is actually what the person should be doing and should be compelled to take advantage of, you will do a much better job.

But here's the reality. Not everybody will buy, even if they should. Only about 20% to 40% of people who enquire will ever buy whatever you offer to them; and maybe not from you either. So make sure that if they are going to buy, you are the person they buy from. This is why what you need to not just educate people but be persistent; something we'll cover in great detail later.

Let me just talk here about the sales situation. Being a great sales person, when you understand this, means you can naturally modify how you operate to be incredibly efficient and take advantage of everything that's going on.

On average, if you're in a room of 100 people, and if you are selling a fairly typical product or service - not something niche - for example say a new car, out of those 100 people about 3 of them, so 3%, are actually in the market looking to buy a new car right now.

But as a sales person you'll be asking the obvious question: "That's only 3% of people. What about the rest of them?" In reality 7% of those 100 people, so another 7, will be ready to buy a new car in the next three months but not actively looking, so they're open to looking at the information and learning about things now, if given the right opportunity.

That's great. We've now moved from 3% to an overall 10% of potential customers in a three-month period. The interesting thing is – and we'll go into this in more detail later – most people will only actually be interested in the sales potential from the 3% of people ready to buy now; they neglect the 7% of people who are ready to buy in the next three months! Just by knowing that and approaching it in a different way - which we'll talk about later - you're in a much stronger position. You're almost feeding your sales pipeline.

So in that room of 100 people there are still 90 people left and you'd like to sell to as many of them as possible, right? In reality 30 are not thinking about buying. Another 30 think they're not interested and the last 30 are definitely not interested.

The people who are definitely not interested you shouldn't waste your time on, so you need to work out who they are fast. The 30 who are not thinking about buying and the 30 that are not interested could still be customers though.

As I said earlier, 20% to 40% of people who enquire will buy over time, but up until now, we've only really invested in the people ready to buy in the next three months, that 10%. But to get more sales than you can handle, which is what this book is all about, you need to highly efficiently continue the sales conversation without investing time, money and effort unnecessarily with the 30% of people who are not thinking about buying and the 30% who think they're not interested.

All of a sudden, you're now dealing with 70% of the market and those are the 70% of people who will bring you the actual sales that you want. As I said, most salespeople are actually only really chasing around after the 3% who are ready to buy now, missing out on 63% of the potential prospects. Having a system in place to target 70% of a market, as opposed to just 3%, is the key to success in sales and marketing.

Success in sales and marketing, targeting 70% of a market not 3%, requires a new approach; one that you are learning in this book. And this new approach starts with how you operate personally, not how a prospect reacts to your sales and marketing efforts, That's why understanding and managing your own behaviour is both critical, but at the same time very easy.

You don't ever get an owner's manual with your brain. Because of this, if you want to be successful, you will need to keep learning and trying new things, for example, going through this book, and applying what you learn from it.

When it comes to it, your results come down to 'state of mind'. As a great salesperson you need to be able to manage your own and your prospect's 'state of mind'. You can actually control that very easily, as we'll talk about later, by auditory, visual and kinaesthetic actions. I won't get into too much detail now; we'll cover it later, but it's important I bring this basic fact up now, especially on a personal level before you get in to selling and marketing.

You have to be confident, too, but not arrogant. Make sure you think about and approach as many things as possible proactively, not reactively, because taking control of a situation and being responsible for making a positive change is, in my experience, the the best way to be confident about what you do and display that enthusiasm and positivity to others.

Here's another thing that's really key for you. You need to be able to spot your own and your prospect's limiting beliefs, the things that are stopping you or them moving forward down the road to a better situation. You have to be able to break those limiting beliefs down. We'll cover that later.

People tend, on the whole, to live in a problem orientated environment. What do I mean by that? They're focused on dealing with day-to-day situations that are problem orientated, for example paying the bills, getting everything done on time, even fixing their aches and pains with pain killers. People are not necessarily looking for a solution-based environment to operate in, because problems dominate their immediate attention, money and time. A good salesperson will help somebody transition away from a problem based environment through the simple act of making a decision and taking action on it: that's a real key skill that we'll cover.

But good is not what we are looking to achieve here and not something to settle for. Great salespeople are willing to do today what other people are not prepared to do, even when it's very easy to do; like make those phone calls, send out those brochures, learn more about the products and services you offer. You get the idea. You need to be focused on doing what other people are not prepared to do today because you know that tomorrow, you'll get the results.

Remember, the goal is not to close every prospect; the goal is to sell and to provide value to everybody who is what I would call 'closable' and who should be sold to. Don't try to close everybody because this will waste a vast amount of your time, your money and your effort. You do this by just doing simple things, like never ducking a phone call or an e-mail, rather responding to them in a timely fashion that suits you, by - if necessary - sending them to your competitor and giving them honest, expert advice. You do this by becoming more approachable and building that rapport, remembering their families and things that are important to them. You must find out what matters to a prospect, what they like and what their hobbies are, because when you start to integrate those things into your sales and marketing, you'll build friendship, you'll build loyalty and you'll become an asset to that person.

One technique to build that bond with your prospects is to use gifts, especially when prospecting. You don't need to spend lots of money, but if you send things that are personal, even a handwritten note, that will be taken really positively by a prospect.

When it comes to writing notes, think about the right language and emotion to use. Don't get overly-friendly, but be personable. Be a real person with real feelings. Have an emotional connection to your prospects because that will show that they know, they like and they trust you.

Although a lot of people try to sell based on features and some sales training and marketing training will say: "Yes, but you need to really focus on the benefits, or the why and covert that into a hook," the reality is - and this is how the human brain works - people are very interested in the why, the benefits, but if you really want to convert people from being a prospect into a customer, the thing they want is the how.

They want to know how, which is great because you can start to feed them with information that helps them understand how things happen, how they can find a solution to their problem, how they can take on an opportunity, how they can profit or how they can take more time off but still get the results they want.

The thing is, what you need to be very clever with as a salesperson, is how to do this; teaching other people, giving them that education, but not by spending so much time, money and effort on them that it's not profitable. Equally, you don't give too much away either.

Too many salespeople are in a situation where people are, as I've said earlier, fishing from them. They want to know how to do something without paying, and that's not good. You need to control that and somebody who's good at sales will be able to do that extremely well. Having a plan and a systemised way of doing it will do that for you and foster the ability to take orders form prospects, not have to sell to them.

Here are some more practical things and some suggestions I'm going to make before we get to the tasks. When you're in a sales and marketing environment, even if you're purely there to sell, you need to spend at least 20% of your time on what's called 'working on something' So strategically, rather than 'working in something', doing it on an operational level or a tactical level (remember the ESTO approach here).

If you need some support as to the sort of companies that do this, probably the best example I can give you is Google, who say to all of their senior employees, their middle management people and the people who really add value to the business, they want them to spend at least 20% of their time at work, for which they are paid, on new developments, on new ideas; not in their day-to-day job. You need to be doing that, too.

You also need to spend, if you're in sales and marketing, at least 25% of your time prospecting. Anything less than that will almost certainly mean you're not getting results because you need to feed the sales pipeline, which we'll talk about later.

To be the best you can be, you need to be relentless, you need to be clever, you need to be entertaining, you need to be persuasive, you have to be compelling and you have to communicate what you do and be a pleasure to deal with. Those are the key factors that sales expert Chet Holmes really drilled in to me and I want you to think about, too. So on that note, we're at the task again.

Remember to make sure you're signed up at MoreSalesThanYouCanHandle. com. There will be some more information and check sheets to help you go through this.

I have five little things for you to do for this chapter:

The first is very simple. I want you to note down the percentage or the number of prospects you currently close. If you were to go out there in a sales situation and speak to 100 people, how many of those would you close?

You might be in a situation where you sell online and you don't have customer contact. I still want to know the percentage of people who enquire in some way, shape or form. That could be visiting your website, it could be putting things in a shopping basket, it could be when you're on the phone to them. Whatever it is how many of those people actually give you money?

Then I want you to answer how many of the prospects can be closed. That's really key, because when you understand that, you can start using the metrics. Remember, I talked about how sales is a numbers game.

I also want you to know, or to try to work out, how many prospects should be closed.

Those are three things that I think are really important, and we're going to build on these as we progress.

Next, I want you to write down what your prospects' limiting beliefs could be. What are the things stopping them from actually spending money with you? Once you know these, you can deal with them.

Lastly, on a personal level, the final question is: what are your own limiting beliefs? When you can identify them – feel free to ask third parties, other people, about this, as well, because that will really help you – you can really transform your results.

# CHAPTER 4

## GET THE SMALL THINGS RIGHT AND BIG THINGS HAPPEN

Getting results fast is about prioritising things correctly and having the basics right. If you just get the basics right, you will make a lot of sales. But to go exponential, you need to be thinking about the payoff from the things you're doing now, could be doing now and how hard it is to do those things so you can get easy, quick wins and continually build momentum over time.

In this chapter, we're going to cover the basics you need to start making more sales. But most importantly, all of these are incredibly scalable, so they will set you up for massive results as time goes on.

As we're getting more in-depth, I want to explain that the key to success is actually not modelling, as most people try to do. The highest profile superstars out there could have been successful partly by skill but partly by luck too.

I'm going to give you what the best 5% do, not what the best 0.5% do. This is minimising - in fact almost eliminating - any risk of somebody being successful through chance and you don't need to take and shouldn't need to take any risks when you're doing things.

Let's talk about selling. What I want to say is that selling is not a battle. People say you win sales. Yes, you do win a battle, but sales is not a battle, it shouldn't be confrontational or a game of one-upmanship.

I've seen this happen an awful lot in a sales environment. What happens is both parties get aggressive, they feel threatened and then they close down. We're looking here for a win-win outcome and, believe it or not, the win actually occurs almost before you start that sales and marketing process.

For example, people like Jordan Belfort in sales or Dr. Chester L. Karrass in negotiation, which is another form of salesmanship, always look to perfect the pitch and sales mechanisms well before they actually get in to actually selling anything. Great salespeople do the research, that way they get it right so when they launch into anything, they're always spot-on right away. All they need to do then is just keep refining their approach. As we say here in the U.K., the Five Ps: Perfect Planning Prevents Poor Performance.

As an example of that, just to give you an idea, I had a meeting yesterday in the middle of writing this. Before the meeting, I did an awful lot of research. I had clearly defined plans. I'd written out things. I created a flow chart as bullet points to go through and discuss.

The person I was meeting with, who actually wants me to work with them and give them money as well as help, said they spent some time researching but actually turned up with nothing and just asked me questions. They didn't add any value to that meeting whatsoever. The reality is, unfortunately for them; their chance of progress is slim to none, which is a shame.

At the end of the day you obviously need to add value to prospects, but if you're the only person adding value to the conversation it's going to be difficult to sell what you offer; though not impossible. However we want things to be easy, not difficult that's why education and building a rapport are so important. Rapport is a two-way thing. All you should need to do to improve your selling ratio is refine your education and rapport building system. That's why the people who work for me in a sales capacity are given what's called a Livescribe pen; something I highly recommend.

A Livescribe pen not only allows you to note down things and make notes from any conversation - that's a the key point here - but as an added benefit people love it when you take notes about what they're saying. The pen also records the conversation in line with the notes you've taken. This way you can go back at any point, re-listen, re-learn, see what works and see what doesn't. This way of working also helps in a non-sales capacity. Remember, sales to me is that transition from being a prospect to becoming a customer. When you have written notes and an audio recording, you can hand that across to somebody to deal with the next step in the process with total confidence, knowing that they have everything they need, even if you've missed something out when briefing them.

Not every prospect you're going to deal with is the same, so you need to be able to customise what I would term a 'Standardised experience' for each person you deal with, if at all possible. By the way, you can do this, no matter what people say, in things like print with digital print and customised printing. You can do it online really easily, in e-mails, and easiest of all, you can do it on the phone or in person. Just by doing this, believe it or not, you're going to differentiate yourself from probably 95% or more of your competition, elevating you into a position of expertise and becoming a trusted advisor, not a salesperson.

People don't actually buy information; what they do is buy results: results that they want. So, before any situation where you're selling - in person or not - you need to know who you're selling to and what the outcome you desire is in the end. Also, you need to know their desire, but not necessarily think that the end outcome is a sale. It can just be taking a step towards a sale.

In terms of understanding a customer, you need to appreciate the customer's 'buying factors,' and make sure those match your strengths, personally and the products and services you provide. If you have any weaknesses - believe me we all have weaknesses as nobody's perfect - you have to minimise the impact of those in the way you manage a sales situation too.

No matter what some people say, it is very important to have a brand, or as some describe it, a commercial personality, because once you build a brand it becomes your calling card and it allows you to charge more for what you do. At the end of the day, we're here not just to make sales but to be highly profitable. So make sure you deal with the branding side.

Also, if it's an in-person situation, you'll want to know who's in that meeting, what they do, what they're responsible for and also what they need to get out of that meeting. Doing this is very easy, just do what I do and ask in advance. If they don't give me the information I need, for example, who will be in that meeting, what they do and what they want to get out of the meeting, I don't go to the meeting because I know I'm almost certainly wasting my time and I'm probably going into a situation where I'll struggle to make a sale. I'm trying to convince somebody rather than compel them to take action and that's not what any of us should have to do.

I actually like prospects to do some work or some research before the meeting because it gets them emotionally invested in the meeting, it saves a huge amount of time and it also qualifies them to me. It means they're serious. It means they actually want to do something rather than, as I said before, get information and fish my brain for information that they can use without paying me.

I tend to give my prospects something to do after a meeting too and if my goal is not for them to give me money at this point in the discussion, I want to make sure that before I come back to them they've actually done that thing I asked of them. It shows they are serious and want to work with me. At the end of a meeting, too many times in a sales or marketing situation, the person doing the selling goes away with lots of things to do, but the person being sold to goes away and does absolutely nothing to do. You never want a one sided discussion or sales process, as mentioned before, especially if you end up with an awful lot of work to do with little or no commitment form the other party or parties; that's a really weak position to come from in a sales context.

I want to sort out time-wasters fast. I don't want to deal with them. I've had many salespeople who were too scared to do that because they really didn't want to put any emphasis on the prospect. But the reality is they didn't make the sales. I take it on the chin, so to speak, but I was paying them too much to start with and gave them too much flexibility. They didn't understand successful sales strategy and they were too soft. It didn't mean they didn't sell, but they were just too soft and they didn't understand what converts the sale, what makes somebody compelled to take action, what engages them, what gets them emotionally involved.

When you are selling - a bit like when you're doing anything, really - you need to do it with enthusiasm. Otherwise, you really shouldn't be doing it. This will also make sure that if you're on the phone, in person or even in a video or any other form of communication, for that matter, you are exuding confidence. Confidence makes the prospect feel like you are worth listening to. It also automatically proves that you know the subject matter and positions you as a guru, an expert and the authority on this subject.

Another misconception is that in sales you should just answer the questions that people put to you. They are what really add value to a situation as it shows you're an expert. But you have to be thinking of almost turning the tables. You need to be asking the questions of your prospects. You need to be thinking to yourself: "What do I need to know in order to do a great job?" Remember, whoever asks the questions, controls the conversation.

On a basic level, you need to really understand the process of what you do, what you sell, whether it's a product or service. But if you just take it on a really basic level, companies like Apple, companies like McDonald's really invest in making sure that the people in front of customers know what they're talking about and know what questions to ask.

Today, for example, I was at an Apple store with my father. He wanted to buy a new iPhone and he asked me to go with him. The sales experience was anything other than sales like and the result was my father went out of the store incredibly happy with his new iPhone. Not only that, in the process, instead of buying the basic iPhone, which is actually what he needed, he was upsold to the most expensive one in the store and he was absolutely delighted to buy it too. He also bought the accessories and everything else to go with it and almost doubled his expenditure.

The Apple store experience was a consultative situation, it was a helpful situation, nothing was too much trouble; but at the same time, the person in the Apple store knew what to ask, how to ask it and to really get to the crux that meant not only was he going to make a sale but he was going to make the best sale he could in the situation.

Here's the thing. When you're selling to other people, they actually – believe it or not – want to gain control of the situation, as that way they feel less threatened. When you ask questions, you can find out what they need to get control of what they're trying to achieve and this will actually help somebody to make a decision, understand and appreciate the value they're being offered. You don't need to sell at that point; you just need to show the value based on the individual's needs, let them feel as if they are in control and let them make up their own mind.

I've heard this described in many ways, but Frank Kern, who is very well known in Internet marketing, uses what he terms his 'Bag of Tricks.' It's exactly the same thing. Frank has in his bag a variety of strategies and tactics that he can pull out based on asking questions and at the end of the supposed sales situation, which is actually more like a consultative discussion or chat, it's very easy for him to close. It's pretty much a done deal before he gets to that close.

In the process of doing that, by asking questions and listening to the answers and using the selection of knowledge you have – that's why it's so important to understand and know what you do, how you do it and add value – you're building a rapport and you get people to subconsciously agree with what you're doing.

A little bit of a trick here, not in a negative way, is if you have something you want to show or explain, as you're talking or writing, drop in to the conversation or onto the page – whatever it is you are doing to sell - a couple of indisputable facts and then drop in your idea, which somebody might question on its own. But the way our brains work means that when you've put your idea after two indisputable facts - and here's the trick in terms of copywriting using a technique called neuro-linguistic programming (NLP) - people will assume because the first two were completely understandable and completely factual, the third one must be, too.

Using the processes I'm covering in the book, you're compelling, not convincing somebody to buy and that requires you to sell for the right reasons and based on experience and emotions, not based on anything else, such as features, benefits or price.

One other thing I see all too often is people selling and marketing to a way-too-wide prospect audience. If you're going to sell to multiple different people in different audience segments, you need to have different strategies and tactics for those different market segments, because not everybody is the same.

People say: "Everybody could use what I do." Well, they could, but you're never going to convince people on that basis. It's way too generic. People, as I say, want to buy from experts. Buyers are pre-conditioned to want to buy from specialists, not people who are generally pretty good at something.

Moving on from that, you need to identify the goals of each of those prospects or group of prospects. As I've mentioned before you need to have a goal that's a bit of a stretch for the prospect, you don't want it to be easy to get as it's not as enticing. You also don't want it to be ridiculously hard to achieve; you need prospects to stretch themselves a little from where they are now. That way, they can see themselves getting there.

One of the major things to realise is that people don't buy for a number of reasons; we'll talk about those later, but one of them is because they don't believe they can get to where you say they can be by buying what you offer. If you just put a little bit of a stretch on the situation, they think: "I could do that," and it's a positive movement, as well.

But when you are setting goals out for yourself or for others, it needs to be specific. All goals need specificity. A goal needs to have a date or a condition attached to it so you can identify how long it's going to take to get there and what's going to happen over time.

You need to identify people, groups, and organisations that align with what you're talking about or you can align with and you also need to identify groups of people who are in your way, as well. Let me give you an example of this because this is really important.

I've had businesses that have not done so well because they've tried to push against a group of people who actually were in the way. One of the businesses I had was involved in a way of connecting print to digital media using what's called a digital watermark, which is actually mathematical information hidden within images.

We were actually working with a lot of publications, a lot of brands and companies such as that, who, on the face of it, absolutely loved it. But when the advertising agencies got involved or the end publications got involved, many of them were very concerned. I'll tell you why. Our mechanism and solution allowed the person spending the money to actually measure the success of a piece of print and agencies and publications didn't want to be measured. The magazine, or the newspaper and the agency placing advertising and PR did not want to be held accountable, or if I was being cynical, get found out.

It didn't matter how strong a pitch we had, how logical it was and how important it was to put some measurement into an industry that was very difficult to measure in real terms; it was very subjective, we were not able as often as we wanted, to actually convert the prospects who we knew should be buying what we were selling, into customers. Media owners and agencies were in the way of us making progress. You need to identify those people and when you do, as we did, you can go around them and make the sales you want. You just change your proposition slightly.

You don't need to take massive action steps along the way to radically improve your results either, but you do need to take action. You need to be able to measure things and that's the thing about goals: they're measurable. You need to have this ability to see what's working and see what's not working so you can change your approach as necessary.

You don't expect the same thing being done over and over again to result in something different happening, so why on earth would you do it in a sales and marketing context? Believe it or not, most people do the same thing over and over again and are bemused as to why the results don't change. It's human logic that things won't change, so make sure you do notice things, you do measure things and you do make changes.

Finally, when it comes down to goals, I want you to understand the reason why a third party is interested in what you have to offer. If you come at goal setting from a prospect's point of view, you'll be able to take your set of goals and modulate them to suit that audience and this in turn shows empathy, understanding, confidence and it demonstrates that you are an expert.

Let's just talk about some basic stats here because I think this is really important before I get to the next part. When it comes to sales, by the way these are not my figures; these are figures that have been developed over time by multiple research studies in to sales. 48% of salespeople give up trying to sell to somebody after one attempt.

When it comes to trying to sell just twice, another 20% give up. Yes, that's right; statistics show that 68% of people in sales and marketing actually give up trying to convert a prospect into a customer after just two tries. That's a crazy situation. I'll tell you more about that in a moment.

Another 7% give up after three attempts. By the time you get to four attempts, another 5% have given up and quit. So realistically, before you actually get to five attempts to sell, 80% of people have given up. This is great news.

Here's the thing. Research also shows that in the U.K. and the U.S., we are exposed to somewhere in the region of 30,000 marketing messages a day and because of that, we've become fairly immune to them.

Before a sale can take place prospects need to recognise and engage with - not just be exposed to -a marketing message, whether it's a brand or a logo, a sales phrase, an image or anything like that, on average at least 7 times - and depending on the research and market segment that figure may rise to as many as 20 - before we take any action on it, let alone purchase. If 80% of people have given up by the time you get to 4 tries, that's pretty damning for sales results because you haven't even reached 7 yet, let alone 20.

What I highly recommend is that number one, you don't give up, because giving up is not a component of success; it really isn't. You need multiple sales and marketing mechanisms and ways to make money, too, because you need to give your prospects so many different avenues in which to take action.

Even when it comes to selling, I want to make sure that rather than maybe selling in person you can sell in lots of ways. You can sell in person, but you can sell over the phone. You can take people's money on the Web. You can even use social media to drive them into sales situations. You can get them to call you. You can go into a physical store. All the ways somebody could give you money, you need to look at in your business to see if they fit and as many as can fit you should be looking to embrace and to use.

So, we've come to the end of this chapter, but we still have some tasks. Make sure you've signed up at MoreSalesThanYouCanHandle.com because there's some information there that can help.

This time your tasks are really simple and there are only two things to do, but they're critical, so don't underestimate them!

The first thing I want you to do is define the sales goals and the measurement criteria from what you currently do.

Second, you need to look at all the sales methods you have in place at the moment and all the ones you could use, and see if you can improve on this.

Once you have those two things in place, moving on will be so much easier and making sales will be so much easier, too.

# CHAPTER 5

# PERSUASION IS A POWERFUL THING

Even though you're looking to compel people to buy, the skill of persuasion is still essential. In this chapter, I want to give you the tactics and the understanding necessary to communicate what you do with prospects in the right way each and every time.

To start with, remember you don't have to accept an order or even market or sell to somebody; this is a very empowering position to come from, without being arrogant. Remember, balancing ego and empathy is really important.

You're also selling what you do, not what a prospect wants you to do and sometimes this doesn't match. Too many salespeople want to agree with their prospects and make changes to what the company does to try to get a sale, but that is absolutely foolish and in almost every case, it's not profitable.

However, I know when I have been asked to make changes for prospects, I've actually charged for it and I've charged handsomely, too. If prospects don't pay well for changes, you just walk away. You want to get to that point of making decision quickly.

I would highly encourage you to listen to what somebody wants, but then, if it's not quite what you do at the moment and they want that change, they have to pay for it or at least give a proper commitment. Don't just go along the lines of "make the change and we'll have a look at it." That just doesn't work.

Let's get into some more subtle ways of persuading. First of all, it's about using tonality. Obviously, the words you use, again more statistics here, are only about 9% of communication. 91% of communication comes from things like tonality and body language. You have to use your tone to build trust and to really emphasise the words you want people to focus on and to draw people in.

I benefit from this: I have an English accent and this works especially well when I used to live in the U.S. and work for a Fortune 500 company. Equally, though, when I do speak – and I spoke at things like the Mobile Marketing Association's conference in New York – having an English accent is incredibly beneficial. I know you can't always rely on something like that, but you have to speak in a manner in which people take you seriously.

All too often, I hear people use the wrong type of language with prospects and that's a silly mistake to make. A good example is pretending you know somebody. This happens all the time at our offices: my father's name is David and the number of times I hear salespeople call up and want to speak to 'Dave'. Nobody who knows him ever calls him Dave. As soon as people in our offices, whether they normally answer the phone or not, hear the name 'Dave' they know it's somebody who is, as we would say, a bit of a 'smart arse' and trying to sell. That's a real no-no.

The tonality and the way you use language is really, really important and that's something you need to think about. I highly recommend you read Oren Klaff's book: 'Pitch Anything.' He talks about something called The Crocodile Brain. You hear that concept in other people's research and material being called a 'Reptilian Brain.' Simply put, we humans have an inbuilt set of responses that protect us and you need to get past that when selling, which just goes to prove we are not naturally inclined to trust sales situations.

One of the great ways to do that is the words that you use and the way you use your tonality. If anybody 'smells a rat' or thinks that's something not right, they get ready to protect themselves. In fact their Crocodile Brain actually does this whether you or they like it or not. The brain reacts automatically to protect you, which means in sales you need to be approachable and non-threatening.

To look at it in a scientific way, I recommend Professor Steve Peters' book: "The Chimp Paradox." He's an individual I greatly admire, when it comes to coaching high-performance Olympic athletes here in the U.K. It's a book I highly recommend and in it, he talks about the 'Chimp Brain' and the 'Human Brain'.

I don't want to go into too much detail because this is not a psychology book, but you need to be able to work with the "chimp" – the fun-loving part of your brain that wants to do things, wants to get excited – but you also need to work with the logical human side too and appeal to both sides of things. That's where having the right communication strategy will really pay dividends for you from both a personal and a sales perspective.

A person will make a split-second decision on any first impression. I believe it's something like one 24th of a second. That is how long somebody will take to making a first impression, and they will do that whether you're there in person, on the phone, presenting information on video, in a letter, a postcard, whatever media it happens to be.

This is where branding is important. As much as some people say: "No, it's not. It's about direct responses, not about branding," Branding is important; but don't overemphasise it. I see way too many people talk about how great they are at sales and marketing, but quite frankly, the quality of their branding work is atrocious. That's a mistake because people make a first impression and rely on it being right for the market later on in a sales situation.

You need to be able to paint a mental picture – whether you're there in person or not – and you get that by having nice, applicable, professional design. Not something overly expensive, not overly complicated, but the right design. You get it by having the right tonality, the right use of words. If you're meeting in person, the way you dress is really important too.

Here's my personal experience on this. I've worked across all sorts of industry sectors and I am traditionally known for wearing a dark-coloured suit, normally black or dark blue, and a white shirt. I take great pride in the way I dress. I don't any longer wear a tie because in virtually every situation now in the U.K., that's not really right, except if I'm working in the financial services sector and a tie is what they expect.

However, as soon as I get involved with the creative industry – for example, media or ad agencies – they wear jeans and t-shirts and trainers to work. Something that I'm a little bit uncomfortable with, I have to be honest, but if I go into that meeting dressed in a suit, I am not one of them, I am not seen as an approachable person. I'm seen more like a bank manager or a lawyer, and that's not what they are interested in and that's not what influences them.

Again, your first impression has to be modified based on your audience. For example, one of the things I try to do is look at where I'm going, if it's an in-person meeting and think: "What are the senior people in that business dressing like? What do the people they look up to dress like?" That's the way I want to dress, so they see me and they associate me with an authority figure in their environment that they're going to work with, learn from, listen to and behave according to their set of rules. That is a really powerful way to make a great and compelling first impression.

Now, moving on from first impressions, you only have somewhere in the region of about three seconds for somebody to begin to trust or mistrust you. Make that first initial contact, in whatever format it needs to be in, really count.

As you move on from that initial three seconds – and let's get this right, so they trust you and you've made a great first impression – I want you to think about having three to five questions that you can ask somebody about their day, because people's favourite subject is themselves.

You can tailor those three or five questions to work-related things; it doesn't have to be trivial gossip, but you goal is to have people to start to open up to you. You want to ask people a question that they are not threatened by and get them talking about themselves, get them talking about an interest they have and to show that you are interested in them and find common ground. That will build a huge amount of rapport almost immediately. As you start to do that, work on being sharp in a really positive way and adding value in the situation, being that authority figure that cares and is helpful.

Another way to really connect with people is using storytelling as a way to explain things. That's why throughout this book, I give you examples from my own personal experience, because they're stories I hope will add value to what you do. I suggest you think about that too in your business dealings.

The other thing - and it comes on from what we've talked about earlier about knowing your prospect - is that I want you to be able to create what some people call a customer avatar and actually work with that. You need to know the profile of the person, what they like, what they dislike; not in an intimate way to start with, but build that up over time and know what your customers are really like.

Also, make sure that in your communication, whatever format it is, you have personality. Way too many situations involve companies selling with zero personality. People buy from people and your ability to show excellence and authority at the same time will not just convince but will influence and persuade people unconsciously; that's a really powerful thing to do.

As I say, selling with a story is great. Somebody I can highly recommend on that front is Kevin Rogers, who was a comedian who turned himself into a copywriter. He says when he is putting together a sales presentation, it's just like creating a stand-up comedy routine and I'm paraphrasing here: 'I start with a problem I've had in the past. Explain how and why it caused all sorts of issues. However, I found out – normally by accident – that by doing something, it sorted the problem out and now everything is great, the problem is gone.' In fact, it's even better than that. Kevin's story telling structure is a very simple structure that really can work in virtually every selling situation, so I highly recommend you see how to apply it for your specific sales and marketing situations.

On top of that, you also want what Chet Holmes, the sales expert, called a 'Core Story'; something based on facts. It also explains your values and the purpose of what you do to a prospect. When you add market statistics and compelling information about a market that maybe your prospect doesn't know, that's really great way to not just provide value and education but stamp your authority and your knowledge on a situation. You'll become an incredibly valued asset to that prospect almost on the spot.

The best way to do, develop and deliver a core story is to start with the scripted approach and you then can start to control things. However, don't have a script that you can't move around. You have to be dynamic; you have to understand the flow of information. Going back to Jordan Belfort's 'Straight Line Selling System', you know the steps people have to go through and that you need to keep them on track; that's why a script is helpful. You also need to be able to manage situations in order to move along that straight line or script, but to be able to deviate as each individual situation necessitates.

Remember, it's not just what you say; it's how you say it. What you need to be making sure is that when you talk, when you're communicating and when you're listening, that you're enthusiastic, you're engaging but you're empathetic as well. At the same time, you need to appear as a figure of authority.

People buy when they love your product or service and they trust and connect with you and your company, when you get all those things right. Persuasion is not only really, really straightforward, it also adds to the whole proposition, the whole value and turns a sales or marketing situation into a really positive experience for everybody involved. No longer is somebody seen as a pushy salesman or somebody they don't want to talk to, you're valued in the relationship and that's what you're looking for.

# CHAPTER 6

# THE RIGHT IINTENTIONS AND PHILOSOPHY ARE VITAL

So far we've covered together some of the factors involved in generating sales and you appreciate that it's vital to manage your own state as well as the state of other people. You also understand that when you're managing a situation, managing states, managing expectations and managing the atmosphere in any sales situation, you need to be able to consistently perform at an incredibly high level. But I want to take things much further and supercharge your results, now you have the basics in place.

Selling is not just a skill used on prospects; it's a skill that's all about adding significant results at each and every stage of running a profitable business. In this chapter, I want to go through some more information, some basic information on the philosophy of sales so that you can apply it to yourself and also to prospects.

First of all, money absolutely matters. If you don't make money and you don't profit, you can't function. It's as simple as that. Money is not a bad thing. Even in a charitable situation, if you can make lots of money, you can give money to charity. If you can make other people money, they will value you.

As John Carlton, the expert copywriter says: "If you are looking for a way to sell without selling, you need to grow up. It's not going to happen". But because of this book, you will not be selling in a negative way. You will be adding value, educating, being a valued resource and an asset. Sell and sell your heart out because that's the absolute right thing to do. Don't be afraid of it.

You also need to remember - we've covered some of this already – that planning and executing great techniques is really important, but to get to that point, don't feel you need to be what you might call 'neat and tidy.' Getting it right is not a 'neat and tidy' activity; it's a creative activity. You need to make notes. You need to get thinking. You need to get those thoughts down on bits of paper and rearrange those thoughts so you can, over time, create a system that you can refine until it really becomes fool-proof. That's what I want for you and that's when you will make massive results happen for you and for your business.

You also need to make sure that what you're doing is making money, but not only that; don't do things that don't make you money or are not close to making money. Everything else is a massive mistake in your situation. As an example of what I mean, let's just look at the child who should be studying for exams but isn't studying: just spending lots and lots of time creating a study guide. It's not helping them get results; it's just keeping them busy.

In sales it looks like this: somebody who should be making sales calls is tidying their desk and sorting their files out in their computer or checking e-mails. These things are not getting you closer to making a sale.

We're all guilty of not using our time the most efficient way we can, there are too many distractions, like the phone, e-mail, social media and things like that, but just realise that distractions are not helping you reach you goals, so you need to manage them and any procrastination you suffer from.

I'm not saying you shouldn't go on Facebook, but don't go on Facebook when you could be doing something that's making you money. Just focus on that and your sales will go through the roof on that point alone.

Also, get things done one at a time and in a logical order. Too many people actually worry about things they're not yet ready to deal with or yet to sort out. This actually causes procrastination and is a great way of stopping you being successful. It's something you'll definitely not profit from. Just do things in the right logical order and make life easy for yourself.

I always say, don't have more than three things that you can start and finish in a short period of time on a to-do list. If you've completed one thing, no matter how small, so long as it's helping you make sales, that's great and it motivates you. If you start multiple things but don't finish any of them it's the opposite. Make sure you do things in manageable chunks that you can deal with, so that you don't ever feel overwhelmed.

Now, when it comes down to the sales situation and the psychology behind it, you need to think about the lifetime value of a customer. That's critical. That way, you can invest more if it's relevant in getting that customer. When you get this right, you can market and sell no matter what the cost of sale is. You can make it profitable.

I'm not going to go into too much detail because this isn't a book about building a business and being entrepreneurial. But, if you know that you can always make a profit and you can upsell, and you can do things entrepreneurially, then you can get as many customers as you want when you have the right suite of products and services to sell. Yes, it's more entrepreneurial, but it's really, really straightforward.

What you need to be getting to, is a point where knowing, for example, that for every £1 you spend on sales and marketing, you're going to get £2, £3, £4 or £5 back. When you know that if you spend a pound you get £5 back, you're going to spend as many £s as you can to acquire customers.

Actually, when I do a presentation or a talk, particularly at events and conferences, one of the things I do is I start by saying to the audience: "Has anybody got a £1 coin?" You normally get one or two people saying: "Yes, I've got one in my pocket."

I then say: "Can I have it?" People usually look at me quite strangely. I then take the £1 coin from them and I give them, depending what's in my wallet at that time, a £5 or £10 note.

Once I've done this once, I then say to the audience: "Has anybody else got a pound?" All of a sudden, the dynamic of that audience changes. Why? Because now, handing over that £1 makes complete sense and that's what you're looking for. That's the philosophy you're looking to get to, where you know that by doing things, you're going to get a profitable, predictable result easily.

When it comes to sales, remember that you need to have values and you need to respect things. You need to respect your prospects as well as your own situation and that will lead to the client trusting what you do, loving what you do for them, loving you as a trusted advisor and trusting the company behind it. That's what guarantees that you get the business and not your competition.

Talking of guarantees, you also want to make sure the guarantee on your product or service is cast-iron. For example, you don't want a debatable guaranteed policy; you want something like a 30-day money back guarantee, no questions asked. Or, if you're selling a car, a five-year unlimited mileage guarantee. Those are things that make people think: "You know what, they're so proud of what they do, they're so confident in what they deliver, they're giving a great guarantee." That is a really solid philosophy that you can use behind your sales of a product or a service.

Talking about that sort of thing, if you're meeting somebody in person, you should make sure that you provide the detail of any guarantee, even if they don't ask; because by doing this up front it singles you out as a trusted – and trustworthy - authority.

Another way to build trust is by keeping eye contact with the person or people you're meeting with. Research suggests that at least 72% of your time in a sales situation requires you to have eye contact with other people if they are to trust you. So don't look at a script or a presentation, know your subject and look at the other people you're talking to. We've all seen people present while reading their notes and I'm sure you'll agree it doesn't suggest they know their subject or should be your chosen supplier, no matter how good the deal on offer.

On the other side of managing eye contact, how many times, when you're talking in person with a prospect, are they checking their e-mail, fiddling with some papers or with their phone? If they are then that's an alarm signal: you're not compelling them to pay attention. Therefore you need to be thinking about your actions, messages, even your mannerisms and those of the prospect too, with the aim of re-establishing a position of authority and getting their undivided attention back.

You need to think about the style and the quality of what you're presenting and talking about. This is neuro-linguistic programming again. You need to use what are called 'matching and mirroring' techniques. You need to play off the people in the room so they feel connected to you.

The things I really want you to focus on are, eliminating certain emotions from your sales and marketing activity because they're negative. You don't want to be seen as greedy. I'm not saying you shouldn't want to make money, but don't be greedy. Don't be selfish. Don't be fearful of the situation.

If there is fear, which is understandable, make sure you understand and accept it. If everything was easy, everybody would be doing it. There's going to be a little bit of fear in any sales scenario. Don't be jealous of a situation either and don't have any doubt in your own mind when you go in to a sales situation. Remember, you know, as far as you possible could, that what you have is right for the prospect. Your only job here is to help them realise that, which is a positive thing.

As I said earlier, make sure you're proud of what you do and because of that, you won't feel guilty when you sell. In fact, you should be really ecstatic because you've sold to somebody and you know it's going to be absolutely the best thing for them.

As you're combining all these things and eliminating those negative aspects, a quote from Walt Disney comes to mind. He said: "You want to combine confidence and you also want to combine curiosity in your sales and marketing" and he's right. You want to combine the purpose and the goals with those clearly defined deadlines we talked about earlier. You need to also combine courage, because as I said with goals earlier, it's really important that you just push out to get to that goal. It's not easy to get there, but it's not ridiculously hard either. You need to be just slightly outside your comfort zone so you need that bit of courage to get there.

Don't worry, either, that people don't always buy. It's inevitable. However, one great way to get people to engage and to buy from you is to create a fear of loss if they don't. People will actually do much more to protect what they've got than to take on a new opportunity. When people feel that and they're ready to buy, believe it or not, they tend to be almost out of control and by buying, they actually feel they're going to get control back and achieve their desired goals. It's a really positive feeling so use that natural positive state we all experience to your advantage.

When you have somebody in not quite a buying frenzy - which could happen - but in a buying situation and they positively want to buy, it's exciting, it's positive and at this point you can upsell and cross-sell far more easily, which is something we've talked about before. That's why you also need to think about the way you follow-up that conversion, right after the prospect has said "Yes". You want to be that added-value person, that person who they want to speak to and deal with again and again so your follow-up needs to be really, really slick.

I would highly recommend you put in place some tools and techniques to keep the customer warm and continue the education process even when they've bought. You will know - as I've already talked about this - that if what you're selling is good for them, it's the right thing to do, and you can then say: "Well, that thing was great and you've really benefitted from that; but what about this too?" Doing this builds that confidence that they have with you. It's most definitely not a bad thing!

You need to be thinking one or two steps ahead of a customer's journey and that's where you'll really, really get the psychology right and make sale after sale after sale. You'll be going back to what I said at the start of this, improving and increasing the lifetime value of a customer. You need to be aware at this point, of what are the next steps that person is going to take; whether they were a prospect or a customer and if there are frequently asked questions or blocking points, you know what they are and how to deal with them, shortening the sales cycle and providing that expertise just when it's needed.

The other thing I also want to say is, you must know what the blocking points to a sale are. If you don't make a sale, understand what the reason the sale didn't occur was and deal with it. You may deal with it by walking away, which is fine if it's the right thing to do, but, Chet Holmes has key strategy revolving around having not just an answer but an action, every time somebody does something positive or negative. Maybe you should too.

For example: if you were doing telesales and somebody said: "I'm not interested," or they just point-blank put the phone down on you, you then need to have a way of reconnecting with them. It might be to send them a piece of direct mail saying: "I tried to contact you about this, but we weren't able to talk, so here it is." That way, you continue that conversation; you continue adding value to a point at which somebody then re-engages with you. Remember, the 7 to 20 times you need to engage with somebody before they take action? You need to have those in place.

And on that, we get to our tasks. Remember, these are all outlined and some helpful checklist information can be found at MoreSalesThanYouCanHandle.com.

The first of the two things you're going to do this time is to make a list of all the possible responses and set-backs you get in any sales situation.

Now, that could be quite a big list, but it's important that you get that list and you add to it over time, and you edit it because as you get better at objection handling, some of those responses won't happen again.

Make a list, get them sorted and then create an added-value response to each of them. Once you do just those things, you will see a huge return in your investment in any sales or marketing situation.

Get them right, take the time to get them down on paper now and refine them over time and your sales will grow exponentially!

# CHAPTER 7

## YOU NEED TO KNOW WHY PEOPLE BUY

There are many supposed secrets to persuasion and the psychology behind it. In fact, many of you may have heard of techniques that I've mentioned before, like neuro-linguistic programming and you may have looked into them, too. But let me get down to the nitty-gritty.

Rather than the glossy descriptions and clever names people use, you should know that you can only persuade or compel people to take action once they've had what should really be called a 'reality check.' That's why information is not enough to make a sale. You need emotion. Better still, if you have the ability to get people to write down or communicate this 'reality check' with a third party, the chance of them taking action sky-rockets.

When people are dealing with facts and they're quite clear on them - primarily because they came to that conclusion themselves and have visualised, vocalised and emotionally connected with them, particularly when involving a third party - they become accountable and stop being influenced by a fictitious situation or indeed what they were hoping their current situation was. They're dealing in facts now and when you deal in facts, you can really make headway in a sales context.

That's why in this chapter, you're going to discover how to get the factual information you need from a market and from individual prospects too; which will result in a huge benefit for yourself and also the customer. This is because of the value proposition that you're always going to put forward in a sales context. It makes prospecting and compelling people to buy far, far easier.

The first thing is - I've mentioned this a little bit before - that people are incredibly self-centred; they're their own favourite topic, which is no bad thing, just a fact of life. We all like to talk about ourselves and what we get up to and our own problems and that's a great thing to have in your bag of tricks, because if you can get people to talk about things in the right way and get to the facts, you can find out how to help them.

Next, people only buy what they want to buy. There's no point trying to convince somebody to buy something that's not just unsuitable for them, but they don't want. If somebody doesn't want something, it doesn't matter how hard you sell or how often you promote to them, they're not going to buy; that's something I see so many sales and marketing people do all the time. So don't try and sell to the wrong people. It's a complete waste of your time, complete waste of your money and complete waste of your effort and to add to that it will not motivate you as there are only so many rejections even the most 'thick skinned' of sales people can take. Only go after people who would want what you offer.

If you're saying: "Yes, but everybody could use what I do," remember that we talked earlier about niching down your marketplace so that you can really focus on what they would want to buy. Don't presume everybody wants to buy what you've got. They don't.

Next, they have to able to afford what you offer. There's no point trying to sell a new Rolls-Royce or Ferrari to somebody who's got the budget for a small city car – Such as a Ford Focus here in the U.K. - They're just not in the market for it and they probably haven't got the money for it, either.

You also have to appreciate that you will only be able to sell if the prospect you're talking to and educating at the same time believes that they can actually attain the outcome you're offering.

There's no point in over-promising, because believe it or not, sometimes it's best to under-promise, so long as the promise is substantial enough for the prospect to take action on. Again, we talked about this a little bit earlier. You want to set a goal for somebody just outside of their comfort zone, outside of their reach, and make them work a little bit to get there because most people don't push themselves too hard. It's too easy to forget that as driven, entrepreneurial people, you and I push harder to get what we want, will work longer, take more risks and be proactive. Unfortunately not everybody is like us and to assume that is a mistake; one which I have made on several occasions when building a sales proposition and marketing to prospects.

If I was explaining to you that in the next ten days, I could show you and work with you to make you a multi-millionaire, you would probably think: "That would be fantastic. I'd love to do that," if you're not already a multi-millionaire. However, you're also probably thinking: "I don't think I can do that. I haven't got the skills, the techniques, the resources, the education," whatever that happens to be and although you'd be wrong in thinking that, you actually do. It would hold you back from taking action.

It's a pretty tall order for you to believe that, in ten days, I can turn you into a millionaire; yet alone a multi-millionaire. It doesn't actually mean I can't, but the chances of you believing me are slim. You have to make sure that your prospect can actually believe they can attain the outcome you're promising in your sales and marketing efforts.

Here's the other thing. The people you're actually prospecting to have to appreciate that you are like them; that you have the same values, the same beliefs and the same attitude of them. Going back to the basics, people buy from those they know, like and trust. It's your values, it's your beliefs and it's your attitude that actually brings those to the forefront and really help you convince as well as compel somebody. They have to feel that affinity to you. Those are some things you have to be really clear on and those are reasons why people actually buy.

The thing is when somebody makes that decision to buy; change for them is almost immediate and actually quite easy. The difficult part is actually getting to the point where they want to make the change, where they take action. That can be a really frustrating thing and it takes time and it takes effort. The reason for this is that you have to break people's habits and habits are something that we as human beings and in fact any animal builds. The reason we build them is that we are pre-programmed to look for ways of making our life simple. We don't want to have to think about things incessantly or actively too often, so if we can form a habit, we'll just go with it until we are really almost forced mentally or physically to change that habit.

You actually have to take the time to help prospects break some non-empowering and negative habits because that's when people can and will change; they'll change fast and actually the change – when they get to it - is quite an easy thing. We've all heard the phrases 'Better the devil you know', 'That's the way I always do it', 'It's just easier that way' and many more like them and these are habit based barriers to making a sale.

When you've got to that right point in the sales situation, remember, the target prospect will buy and actually they'll really enjoy buying. You're not being pushy, they're really compelled and they're ready to do the deal at that point. And talking about buyers, as opposed to prospects, there are basically two buying types of person. We all exhibit an element of both of these characteristics, but depending on what we are in the process of buying; we tend to be more angled towards one or the other of them.

The first one is what I would call a Hedonistic buyer: somebody who gets really excited. They're proactive and want to take action. This is my dominant buying personality. The second is an Arithmetic buyer: somebody who's quite logical and thinks through things. These two buyer personalities are why it's really important that, in your sales and marketing pitches, you work out how to deal with, simultaneously, the Hedonistic side and the Arithmetic side.

You'll recall I've talked in the past about how a sales situation needs to have lots of benefits. You need to get people not necessarily excited but keen on making a change. As I mentioned earlier about the Chimp and the Human brains, the Hedonistic side is very Chimp-orientated, it's really excited but can be quite short term. Everybody has this influencing them; that's also why the right headline or image is so important in sales and marketing material. So to maximise you results you need to back that up that Hedonistic characteristic using the Arithmetic side, even if it's less powerful and persuasive for a buyer because when they say "Yes", they're thinking, "You know what, this is a logical purchase too."

Yes, people will be driven more by either being Hedonistic or Arithmetic, but when you combine the two, sales are so much more simple and people are so much more compelled to buy from you. It's almost funny how easy things go.

You see, people will buy into your goals but actually, what they'll really support and become a fan of is a vision. People really connect with visions, so you need to set out your offer as a vision for them and get them to experience it in their mind before they go ahead and buy. This way you're emotionally and mentally getting them involved in the process. For example, if you were to sell a holiday, you want your prospect to experience, in their own mind, what that holiday would be like, the memories they will have. To do this, use techniques such as neuro-linguistic programming and assume they're going to go on the holiday you are proposing. Never assume that they're not going to do things or ask them if they're going to do things; this is negative and does not focus their attention on the outcome and the vision you have for them.

Say to them: "Once you've had that holiday, you'll be able to look back and remember the great times you had, the events in which you took part, the things you experienced and the new people you met." Get them to connect to a vision of what that experience is going to be in their mind.

Remember, if you're going to try to sell to people who don't want it, can't afford it and are not motivated and don't have the belief that they can get to where you're showing them they can go, you're wasting your time. Almost 100% of it. Think about the way you present what you sell, whether it's a product or a service so you can get those things in play.

Now, in this section, in this chapter, I want to provide you with a task. The best task I can provide you with comes initially from a highly respected marketer called Dan Kennedy, whose expertise lies particularly in the area of direct response marketing and he's very well-known for copywriting too.

In this task, I've given you Dan's ten questions, because once you have these and you can answer them, it will make putting together the things I've covered with you so much easier.

Now, you quite often hear Dan Kennedy and others who use this technique talking about finding 'irrational customers'. These are people who have an irrational passion or need. Such people are really easy to sell to. You're not necessarily going to be in that situation, though, so don't worry about finding people who are so passionate about a subject that they have to take action. It's not going to be that case for everybody. But, these ten questions are really powerful, so I want you to go through them and remember you can go to MoreSalesThanYouCanHandle.com and get some more information there to help you. I want you to be able to answer these and honestly answer these, not make up what you think the answers are or should be, because once you have these ten things down, it's going to make a massive difference to you.

1. What keeps your prospects awake at night in the market you serve?
2. What are your prospects afraid of?
3. What are your prospects angry about, and who are they angry at?
4. Which of their top three daily frustrations can you help resolve?
5. What trends are occurring and will occur in their business lives or if you're selling to them personally, their personal lives?

6. What do they secretly, ardently, desire most?

7. Is there a built-in bias to the way they make decisions, and if so, what is it?

8. Do they have their own language or phrases that are used over and over again by them and those who are selling to them? (When you know these, you can use them, too.)

9. Who else is selling something similar to them and how?

10. Who else has tried to sell them something similar and how had that effort failed? (Again, once you know why somebody else has failed, you can resolve that in your sales marketing pitch.)

Now, I want to add a couple more questions onto these, which I know will be really useful for you, as just those ten, to me, are incomplete. My two questions are:

Who else is selling to your target market a non-competitive product?

Knowing this will be really useful and we'll come back to this later, but, for example, if you're targeting an affluent market, you can see who else is selling to them and what they're saying and doing to get them to buy.

Also, as the last question, I want you to try, as best you can, to define the following:

In your specific situation how long it takes for somebody in your chosen marketplace – whether it's a product similar to yours or not - to go from being just a cold prospect to being an actual customer.

Again, once you've analysed that, you can sort things out in your own system to really take advantage and minimise the cost, the effort and the frustration.

There you are! There are Dan Kennedy's ten questions and a couple more I've added on the end. Have a go at these and we'll keep going and moving forward in the next chapter.

# CHAPTER 8
## GETTING THE FOUNDATIONS RIGHT

With any situation where acquiring and maximising the value of customers is taking place, you must be focused on getting the foundations right. Because when these are in place and solid, you can build a substantial business on them without fear of it collapsing. Let me take you through my own customer foundation building principles so that you can put them in place for your own situation and client base.

Customer value and the customer's point of view are always the way you should look at things, but the reality is that less than 10% of products or services seem to try and sell this way; which is great news for you.

For example, just yesterday I was at a trade show and I had to laugh (internally obviously) when the man on the first trade show stand I stopped at, said to my colleague and I, something along the lines of: "We do this, we do that, we're great at this..." and so on. At no point, did he address the situation from our point of view as the prospect.

Later on, as I was walking down one of the aisles, I saw a brochure on somebody's stand and it was actually called '101 Great Things About...' The name of that company followed, but I'll not tell you who it was. If that is not self-centred, I don't know what is. The reality is, it's quite funny to me, but it is, in fact, hurting a company's ability to get prospects to part with their money and at events like trade shows, the cost of being there is very high, so you want to maximise the return on that investment.

Now that we have that absolutely right, you need to be looking at the things you can work on and the things you can influence - not the things you can't - when it comes to sales and marketing. Too many people are bothering to spend time on things they have absolutely no control over, so I want you to be thinking about the things that you can influence and you can deal with.

Think about things like the leads you get, the way you do cold calling if you're into the telesales side of things, the direct mail, the meetings that you have, and the responses that you get from people. We've already talked about how you respond to things even when it's less than positive or not what you want to happen and also how to influence the actual sales themselves. The way I recommend you do this is to structure what you do based on my ESTO philosophy – Entrepreneurial, Strategic, Tactical, Techniques and Tools, and then Operations.

What I have here is a diagram for you and it shows you how to work from the core component, which is the "E" – the entrepreneurial side – and then, as you get into Strategies, Tactics or Operations, where you branch off those.

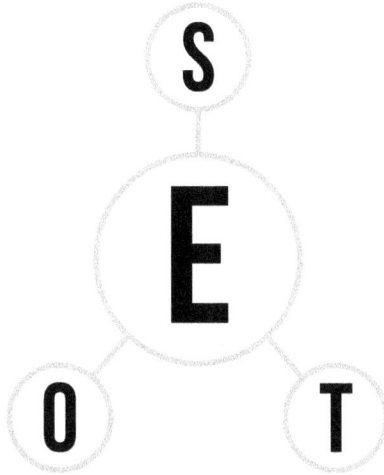

Next, your thinking needs to be based on the actual part you're in. For example, if you're in the tactical area, where many of the day-to-day components of sales and marketing occur, you may have three specific things to work on and having these distinctive will help when it comes to evaluation, accountability and making regular improvements.

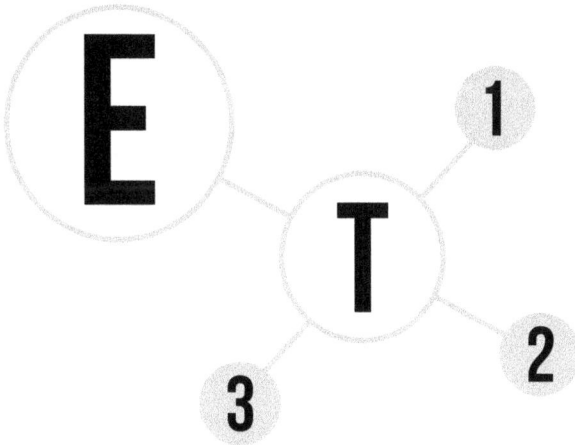

When you're actually doing your sales and marketing, and getting the foundations right, you can think to yourself: "The core component here is the Entrepreneurial part - what makes you different?" You have the strategic part, but in the Tactics or Tools, think about the elements or tools that are required by that – each individual thing – and separate them out. When you do that, it gives you a really solid base and it stops you confusing one from another. Think about the particular elements or processes that are at play in your particular branch of ESTO.

To continue on from that, one thing that I can categorically say is true of all successful people, no matter what they do, is they have targets. The best ones, particularly in sales and marketing, have daily targets, not just weekly, monthly or quarterly as you would normally find in a sales scenario.

Getting things right and keeping things really simple, for example, how many new prospects you can attract a day, is something that is very easy to measure. But more importantly, if you have daily targets, you can see in an instant, if you're veering off course, if what you're doing is working or not working, and take immediate action.

You also need to be thinking. For example, let's say you have a target of getting four new prospects per day. If you're consistently getting five or six, that's fantastic, but then up your expectation, up your target to that five or six, because you never want to be stagnant, you always want to do better. That is a real key to being successful and getting the foundations right. It's that desire, that passion and that energy level that comes from being successful and matching or exceeding your targets.

Now onto some more basic things like education. We've talked about sales happening when people are educated and know and understand what they need to do. We'll go into that much more, later on. A good example I'll give you here to look at is Gary Vaynerchuk's book 'Jab, Jab, Jab, Right Hook', in which he talks about how you give away three pieces of educational content before you ask to sell anything. That is a simple but great general approach. I see so many people in the sales and marketing context trying to sell all the time, whether it's online, on the phone or whatever; it's a really negative thing. I'm going to cover education more later on, but that's a foundation that you need to get right.

You also need to be able to share your vision and make it the prospect's vision, too. Think about that. What is your vision for the transformation they're going to get? What is that particular prospect's vision? Make them match up. Share the vision because that will work for you. Remember you're looking to find problems that prospects have and new opportunities that will open up for them, because that is what they'll buy into.

Here's another one. Before you start pitching to anybody, make sure you're pitching to the right person and know who that person is. If you are the sort of organisational person who does cold-calling, and quite a lot of people actually like doing cold-calling - it's not for me, but people do - you're highly unlikely to get things to work if you don't speak to the right person.

I had an instance just today where somebody was on the phone and they were trying to sell me something that, fundamentally, I was not interested in. They actually phoned up and asked for the wrong person. That's not going to help in a sales situation. It's certainly not going to help when they want me to take a meeting; they don't know my name, they haven't asked anything about my business and they haven't even told me what they do. All the sales person tells me is they're seeing somebody around the corner from me and they would like to come in and have a meeting and tell me all about what they do. When I asked him what his company does, he didn't want to tell me over the phone because he needed to do it in a meeting. You can guess the meeting didn't happen, he didn't get my name and details and we certainly will not be doing business together.

Moving on from that, you need to understand the price you're going to be able to charge is not based on getting somebody to find the budget. You need to be thinking that the money you're charging a client or a customer is based on the future results, not on what money they have today.

Most people nowadays don't have spare money 'kicking around'; they have to look at what they're going to get in the future. If you can tie what you charge into future returns – and better still not take that money until they've started to get those results - you are going to find it far easier to make sales.

Remember if you're going to fail or if you're not going to get the sale, you want to fail quickly and, as Google say, you want to fail forward. Fail fast and fail forward. By forward, they mean by learning something, by benefiting, by being able to refine what you do so you don't make that mistake again; because it saves time and it saves money.

Remember, we're looking for this 'know, like and trust' element. One way that I recommend you do this is by reading a book called 'The Dan Sullivan Question' and applying what you learn. Dan uses what he calls the R-Factor Question. I'm not going to go through the logic and background with you because it's Dan Sullivan's material and I really want you to buy the book, it's very inexpensive and it's really powerful, but you should know, Dan Sullivan's the founder of Strategic Coach and he knows a thing or two about being successful. Basically, the R-Factor Question gives you the ability to see if somebody is forward-looking, that way, you are able to show them a future that they can look forward to. If they don't have that characteristic, it is going to be very difficult for you to work with them and sell to them. That is why it really ties in with what I said earlier about the price you charge for what you do being future-based and not about finding money today.

Remember, you're looking to measure things but so are your customers. They want a return on their investment. By giving prospects something that is very clear, with measurable benefits, you can show them the numbers and provide them with certainty and a scalability that they need in order to say "Yes" to your proposal, no matter how you make it.

Also, this is where you need to look at how you work and I suggest you work, with what I would call a funnel. With a funnel approach, potential prospects come in at the top, you then validate them as to being, as we've said earlier, the best type of buyer for you, and over time you take them on the journey in which they become customers. Obviously, you need more people in the top of the funnel than come out the bottom, but that's logical and can be systemised.

Now not everybody who enters your funnel will buy. However, you can look at your return on investment and by doing this improve that funnel, so instead of being cone-shaped - wide at the top and narrow at the bottom - you can change that so that you get more people in the funnel but convert more of the percentages. The funnel changes shape to be closer to tube.

Being in a position to make changes effectively and efficiently was the reason I developed the ESTO principle, as it's a really clever way to do anything in business, not just sales and marketing. It gives you measurable elements throughout the process that you can modify, refine and can keep an eye on to make sure you're making the most of your time, money and effort. The most costly part of any sales or marketing activity is getting new customers; so you don't want to waste them. Remember, that return on investment shows that people act in a logical way. They're not random human beings, so treat them as logical people, don't treat them on a random basis because that will not help you sell.

Something I see salespeople do all the time is chase turnover. You must stop this culture as soon as you spot it. Chasing turnover makes people busy and foolish at the same time. You need to be really focused on the profitability of a customer across the whole lifetime of that customer, whether that is a single sale - which I don't recommend but may be the only potential outcome - or multiple sales across time, be it a short period of time or many years. You want to build that lifetime customer value and make them as profitable as possible.

One thing I know in any industry, whether you're selling high value things or very low value things, is that you need to think about that lifetime value. When you get the mechanics right, this is more into the Entrepreneurial and Strategic side of the ESTO principles. You can afford to spend an awful lot of time, money and effort acquiring customers. The biggest win you can find is being in a position where you have such a great system in place that you can make money and therefore, you can spend more money than any of your competitors acquiring new customers. This will not only drive your sales up exponentially, it will really hurt your competition too. The more you hurt your competition, the more they'll struggle and maybe even go out of business, which gives you even more ability to profit.

On that basis, you want to reverse engineer things. You need to know your numbers: the market audience size, the number of calls you make, the meetings you attend, and the sales you make. You need to be thinking, as I put it, like the X-Factor TV show. You need to take a huge pool of people to start with and funnel them down every single week, so at every stage, you sieve them out until you get a winner or a really good group of people.

With the TV show The X-Factor, they've reverse engineered a system that allows them to come out at the end with somebody who is a marketable proposition; who they, as a business, can sell and profit from. Forget the fact that they're making money out of the TV shows, the merchandising and all the rest of it; Simon Cowell has created a system for profiting, and the system is based on starting with a massive audience of potentials and drilling them down into the right few that make a lot of money. That is why even people in the X-Factor who don't win it - for example, One Direction - can be global superstars, because they've gone through, believe it or not, a business, marketing and sales funnel that is highly controlled and has metrics and measurements from not just the experts, being the panel, but also the public. That is a really great way to look at what you do. Even though you might not be looking for the next One Direction, there is no reason why you can't use that technique for sifting and funnelling from prospects through to customers.

In terms of another thing I want to call out here, we talked earlier about Jordan Belfort and his "Straight Line Selling System", where the quickest way to get from prospect to a sale is a straight line. This is completely right and is true in every situation for anybody, no matter what their experience is of sales or what their experience is of a market that they want to buy into. You need to be thinking about the goals along that straight line, and you also need to realise that "yes". The principles are the same on that. However, as we said earlier, everybody is unique and individual so you have to manage and control each situation to keep prospects on track.

There used to be an old sales model that was in play and it's something that people still use today, although I don't believe it's the right way to sell. I'll tell you why in a moment. Basically, there used to be some statistics that said in a sales model, 10% of your time and resources need to be put into building a rapport with somebody, 20% of your time needs to be into qualifying that prospect, 30% of your time needs to be about presenting to that customer or prospect and 40% of your time should be spent trying to close that prospect and make them a customer. That really doesn't work, because if you're spending 40% of your time closing, you're spending 40% of your time trying to convince somebody to give you money.

What has happened is there is a newer consultative selling model that is much closer to what you really should do and goes like this:

10% of your time or resources are invested in confirming and closing a customer. By 'confirming', I mean making sure they should buy because when you do that, the close is an automatic situation. It doesn't require you to try and convince.

20% of your time needs to be put into presenting solutions to people. Not doing a presentation, but giving people solutions to their situation, their problems, and showing them opportunities.

30% of your time needs to be invested into identifying the needs, so that way, you're only presenting solutions to people after identifying their needs, this really cuts down on waste.

40% of your time needs to be put into building those relationships. The time doesn't actually need to be face-to-face or on the phone, it could be done online, it could be done through a case study, it could be done through trade shows. Building relationships is not just a one-to-one situation. You can, when you've structured it correctly in sales and marketing, deliver what I call a one-to-many situation. For example, think about it as if you were standing on a stage in front of 10,000 people. You can build a relationship from that stage with all 10,000 people at once. Equally, you could create something like a video presentation online and, again, you will be able to connect with hundreds or thousands of people without going to hundreds or thousands of meetings.

As a personal example, I've created all sorts of online training materials; one in particular is all about goal setting. As a test, I put that onto a website called SlideShare. Within a month of putting it on there, I actually had over 10,000 people watch a presentation that I created in PowerPoint and converted into a little video. It took me about 20 minutes to create that, yet I had over 10,000 people watch it. As a consequence, I was able to build a relationship with many of those people without ever meeting them. So you see a one-to-many can be highly profitable when you have the backend system in place to take advantage of it.

Think about this concept of consultative selling, as we've covered, but think about it with seven steps in mind (I'll come to those in a moment) to really make the best use of the sales opportunities out there today. What you need to be doing is thinking in this order about attracting customers, establishing a rapport, and finding that need. We've covered building relationships, identifying needs, presenting solutions scenarios in there, building value with that audience, creating that desire and compelling them to take action. You need to overcome objections and then you need to close. Once you've closed, that is not the end. You need to follow-up. You need to deliver added value nowadays, even when they've said yes and have paid you money.

As I said, there are seven steps and you should do them in this order:

1. You need to attract prospects

2. Establish rapport

3. Find a need

4. Build value

5. Create desire

6. Overcome objections (as these are opportunities to educate)

7. Do business and follow-up

If you're not doing business, you need to look at your whole system and maybe even get out of sales, because as we said right at the start, everything you do, every word you say, is about doing business, or as some say closing. If you're selling a quality product or service to somebody who needs it - and you are, at the end of the day, goal-oriented - you're not here to have random conversations with people - you're here to make sales.

On that basis, here are the tasks. There are a few in this one, so I'm not going to hide from the fact that, as you go through these, you are going to build up some incredibly powerful material and knowledge that you can apply to really transform your results. It's not a five minute job. However, the first task is!

Number one: I want you to spend no more than five minutes in writing out a brief background, an overview of your business and the products or services that you offer so that you could share that written brief with anybody, even if they didn't know anything about you, and they would be absolutely clear on what you do.

Next, I want you to write down what differentiates you from your competition. What are your business's core values? These are key to the sale remember; if they're not, they should be, so I want you to get that down too.

Next, in a perfect world, I want you to be absolutely clear on what you believe that you can accomplish for your customers. Again, if you know where you need to get to and you know where your client needs to get to, you can really hone in on that and do a fantastic job for them, adding value and becoming an asset to them rather than just a supplier.

I also want you to note down who the influential brands in the market or space you serve are and who you admire, who you fear and who you don't admire or fear too as this is not only interesting but useful to know.

Now go out and find some market research or insight that you could give to a prospect that they would find useful and actually supports what you're selling.

Next, I want you to define what your core offering is: your 'flagship' offering. What is the best thing you can do for somebody?

At the same time, what is the most profitable thing you can do? Your core 'flagship' offering should be highly profitable.

I also want you to then make a note of all the non-flagship offerings you do, because these are what some people call profit maximisers. Sometimes they are a way to get people to buy who are maybe not ready for your core offering.

From there, I want you to look at and make note of how you're generating the bulk of your leads and your customers. I want you to also know how many leads you're getting every week, every month or whatever is relevant for your business.

Next, I want you to describe your customers and I want you to describe them demographically; things like their age, their sex, where they are geographically and also their psychographic side. This is more about their behaviour, what they like, what they do with their time.

Next, I want you to be clear, based on what you've just described from your current customers if you've got them: is this actually your ideal customer? If it's not, you need to fully explain, in your own words, on a piece of paper, who should be your ideal customer and again, have a demographic and psychographic profile of them. Remember, we're talking here about your best prospects, your highest value customers, the people you actually want to do business with; not necessarily the people you are doing business with.

Next, I want you to define what you could do, say or give somebody that will in maybe three to five minutes, give them what I call a quick win, or, some people say, will 'blow their mind'. What could you do for somebody that gives them results in advance and they go, "Wow, that was really impressive." When you know that, you can implement it and you will have sales coming at you at an incredible rate.

Next, you need to know what the one big thing that your prospects want more than anything else is. You may well find even in a business-to-business context, it is a personal aspect, so have a think about that.

Next, what other products and services do you have that you haven't talked about or written down yet? Make a list of them so you know and you're clear about each one of them.

Now from there, think about how do you and how could you follow-up with customers and prospects? I highly recommend here that you look at how you can either automate these, using things like e-mail auto-responders, direct mail or things like that. This way you put a system in place so there are no 'grey areas' or any chance it's not followed. For example, you knew if somebody called, then again two days later. This is what you do even if it's a manual task, and this is what would be communicated.

Next, define what your current sales cycle is, how long it takes, what things are in there. Once you know, it's very easy to monitor it and to perfect it.

Only two more to go! What is the most expensive or amazing thing you can or could do for your customers? Remember, we're talking about the ESTO principles. I need you to be starting to think on an entrepreneurial level, so I want you to think about what you can or could do for customers that may be even more expensive or even more amazing than your core product at the moment.

Finally, make a list of anything else you think that you may find useful because that will really help you in moving forward. As we keep going in this book, I think you're going to build on these incredibly well and start to see results really fast.

# CHAPTER 9

## FINDING THE RIGHT PROSPECTS

I've worked in marketing-oriented situations for almost 25 years now and was brought up in a household where a sales and marketing agency was the main family business, so I really have been there, done that, got the t-shirt and have the battle scars, too.

From a cost point of view, I've created literally thousands of campaigns using tactics as diverse as e-mail marketing, social media and small run digital direct mail, all the way through the other end of the cost scale, like TV ads, Formula 1 team sponsorship and international trade shows. This really is my forte and should soon become yours, too, if it isn't already.

You recall in the last chapter, I covered the seven steps you need to take. They were:

- Attract

- Establish rapport

- Find the need

- Build value

- Compel and create desire

- Overcome objections with education

- Do business and then follow up

Therefore, in this chapter, I want to talk about attraction; because until we find the right prospects, you're making life harder than it needs to be. To accompany this chapter rather than it becoming a book in its own right, I've provided more at the website, MoreSalesThanYouCanHandle.com, in terms of a video running through how to get more customers. It's over an hour long and has 85 different tactics that you can use; no matter what money you have to spend, to attract best buyer profile customers across all media types.

Everything you need to know first of all about your market and what's working right now is out there online and can be researched in a few hours, either by yourself or by somebody else. It amazes me how many of what I would call 'idiot sales calls' I get because they don't do any research at all. Believe it or not, a little bit of research online is probably the best and most profitable use of the internet once done correctly, yet it's one of the least leveraged.

You want to focus on small manageable targets. Depending on what business you're in, a small target might be 10 people, 20 people, 100 people, or 1000 people based on your own personal situation. But you need to communicate with these people on a consistent basis. Too many times, I see people target too many people, which will inevitably lead to no action.

Remember, you have to communicate with people maybe seven or 20 times before they'll take any action. If you want to try and target 1000 people a time without the right systematic approach, you're going to find it really difficult to get them to engage with you and to take that action. You're now, because of what you've learned so far, working in what I call 'campaigns', not events and this fits with the S component, the Strategic component of the ESTO system. let me explain.

A campaign is multiple items joined up and strategically delivered. People tend to do sales and marketing and advertising and PR and things like that as one-off events. That's a major mistake. It will not work for you and will really limit your activities and your results. You need that joined-up thinking that strategy brings and a campaign is multiple communication pieces, multiple adverts and multiple bits of PR all done together with a single goal. We'll talk a little more about that in a bit.

In terms of that, people tend to hire or have different suppliers for different events. They might have somebody who does PR, somebody who does their digital marketing, creates their website, does a bit of design work, they might go onto somewhere like Fiverr to get a logo created, all sorts of ways to do wonderful things. There's no problem at all with that; however, if you do not have a joined-up cross marketing and cross-media approach behind it all, you're making a major mistake.

You need to be clear on that strategic message that you need to put across everything you do. Remember you need to be thinking about the direct response component and the branding across everything, not just single events. It needs to be consistent because that's when you'll get the best return on your investment.

Another bit of advice here is to go and get a calendar, preferably one you can write on, not an online or electronic one. Plan your campaigns and each event in the campaign and write them on the calendar. Get really organised in advance whenever you possibly can. Too many people almost think: "I'm going to do some prospecting or some marketing or advertising when I'm quiet." That's not going to be useful to you. You need to have an ongoing plan, know what happens when it happens and what happens next after that and why.

In certain businesses I'm involved in, we really do have not just a calendar but we have multiple things happening every single month across all media formats and it's the core part of the business. We can actually run sales teams of over 100 people based on those calendar-based activities and you can be doing that too.

You don't need to have, as we do in certain businesses, more than 100 sales people and a big budget to spend. You can have just a small business that do yourselves and you do your marketing as part of that. But as soon as it's on the calendar, you can plan in advance and get things organised. However, don't organise too far in advance. Remember, you're monitoring and measuring everything, so you want to plan, but you also want to be able to modify when you find out something new and refine the process to get the best results and the best return on your investment. How do you go about doing this?

The first thing to do is to look at the three to five most common questions people have about what you do and answer them. Remember, we're talking about education-based marketing. As I said earlier, you need to balance direct response with brand building in what you do. Let me give you more of a description about these two things.

Direct response is all about getting people to take action. They're being proactive, they're improving their education and they're doing it virtually risk-free. If possible, you need to deliver that education, that direct response component at virtually zero cost to you as well as to your prospects. Then when they come and are educated, they're almost self-selecting and they become best buyers or great prospects. Imagine having to educate all prospects on a one-to-one or going to meetings, then come up with a strategy to do this without personal time and money invested. Remember the one-to-many approach I mentioned earlier.

One of the things I've had to deal with, in certain circumstances, is sales people that continually go to meetings to do education and wonder:

(a) why they're not making sales because they're having to spend all their time educating people and (b) why they don't last in the role very long because on top of not making sales, their cost to the business is astronomical. You needn't do this when you use direct response principles correctly.

But at the same time, you need to be brand building, again, something that so-called 'gurus' totally fail to deliver on, or understand, in some cases. By having a brand and a positive brand as a by-product, it means you get better recognition over time, higher sales over time and can increase your prices over time, too. The reality is brand building is just all about good design, good images, consistent messages across all your media and presentations and delivering the right quality of material for your market.

For example, people get carried away by having award-winning material in their marketing, advertising, PR and everything else. The reality is that an awful lot of scenarios do not need that. If you look at very successful websites, for example, Amazon, they are not going to win creative or artistic design awards; they are however winning a heck of a lot of business because the quality and the design and the material and the content is spot on for the markets they serve. Amazon will happily trade a pretty website for a profitable one and I suggest you do too.

You need to get branding right, so if somebody says that you don't need to invest in good quality photography, video, design or copy, they're wrong; absolutely wrong. They're looking very short term and that's a mistake that you don't want to make.

In your market, you actually want to build a brand; position yourself differently but at the same time, take advantage of direct response principles. That's something I do not only for my own businesses but for corporates, too, who don't tend to understand the direct response part. They have agencies that are spending a vast sum of money on brand building. When you combine the two, it's incredibly powerful and effective for your return on investments.

In terms of attracting people, you want to attract people based on a personality because that's the positive way to do it. You want to be thinking about engaging with prospects, as if you are talking with them, not taking to or at them. I recommend that you use what they call a 'squeeze page' on websites to capture information. That way, you can continue to engage with prospects and build likability and trust. By having a personality, you will either attract or repel people, which is a really great way to self-select and find those best buyers.

When it comes to lead capture or prospecting, there are two ways to do it. You have what I call the Shotgun approach or the Sniper approach; you need to be aware of this and the potential of both approaches, depending on a specific need. Here's how you market to those different approaches – again, something not very many people understand or talk about.

Let's talk about the Sniper approach to start with. This is where you get very target-specific in your message and the way you promote. Sniper approaches can work in all sorts of ways. For example, direct mail, e-mail marketing, advertising on Facebook; things like that. You have very much a target audience and you're actually approaching a small number of people. In a sales context, it could be picking up the phone on a cold call; it could be knocking on a door or asking people specific information. But fundamentally, you're not trying to appeal in your message to thousands of people all at once; so you have to take what I call a Sniper approach to that message and you have to make it very personal and very relevant to the individual. That way it will work.

However, the other side of the coin, and this is what most brands do, is the Shotgun approach. If you're using the Shotgun approach, which isn't actually wrong, you're goal needs to be to capture the attention of as many relevant people - I'll say that again, relevant people - as you can. This is done by doing things like changing the headline or making the call to action different, so you're capturing lots of information. You can then start filtering that down automatically with things like e-mail marketing or more retargeting when it comes to your online advertising.

For example, when you're using a Sniper approach you might send a single piece of direct mail, which may have a cost of let's say £1.50 with the print, the message, and the postage. However, a Shotgun approach could be an advertising piece in a national magazine, and that could cost you £10,000, so you have to have a different approach to get the right return on investment.

What you should be using your Shotgun approach for is to capture lots of targets to then drill down to being able to deliver a more Snipered approach to individuals. But what you should also make sure with a Shotgun approach is the way somebody appreciates that what you've presented to them is in a very much one-to-one communication style. Don't talk to people en masse; talk to people on a personal level. Again, going back to that personality I talked about earlier and attracting people on that personality basis.

The other thing to think about when you're marketing, whether it's Sniper or Shotgun, is what I call picking your weapon based on the media and the return on investment model. The return on investment, obviously, is based on the cost of it, but as I tend to say, don't take a knife to a gun fight; but do take a gun to a knife fight.

What do I mean by that? If you're going into an environment where, let's say, people have lots of money to spend, then I call that a gun fight. You have to go in there with something that can deal with other people in the market with guns, with budget. It doesn't mean you have to spend an awful lot, but you have to be very clever.

You have to go in there with the right ammunition, the right machinery, the right backup and the right systems in place; which in fairness, most big brands don't have. They just have big budgets, so you can compete with them for much, much less when you know how.

However, if you go into a big market where big brands are spending big money with what I would call a knife, which is basically something not done very well, doesn't produce the professional branding and appearance that market expects, then you're going to fail.

Big brands and big organisations make the mistake of not speaking to people on an emotional, one-to-one level in most cases and also try to create an average product or service for average people. They never become the best at something specific; that's your opportunity because people want to be treated like an individual.

I'll use the Shotgun, Sniper and weapon-type analogy here again just to say, make sure that if you're going to go into a gun fight you take a gun, and a good one too, but if you're going into a knife fight and you have a gun, you're chance of winning is very high, almost inevitable and that's I want to deliver for you, a gun that can help you win any fight. That's why I wrote this book and created the videos and support material on the website. By using it all and doing the tasks I have set, you can absolutely do that.

Another thing I want you to think about is joint ventures and partnerships because they're a great way to work and it really reduces your cost of acquisition of customers, even if you have to pay a commission to people.

Now let's go into a more systematic approach to sales, as this will boost your results and minimise your costs. When you've started to attract someone, think how to automate the follow up and systemise things. I really suggest to people that they systemise things for at least 30 days, maybe even up to 12 months depending on your market and your sales cycle. You can do things with e-mail, you can do it with direct mail, you can do it with a catalogue, brochures and things like that. But having that 30-day plus automatic solution in place means that you can communicate with people easily 20 times and get them interested in what you do or sift them out with very little or no overhead.

Remember, while you do that, you need controls and measurement in place in all your attraction methods. But remember also that you should have multiple attraction methods, not just one. At the moment, if you're just generating new business leads by let's say direct mail, you need to be thinking about how you can take what you've learned in direct mail and apply it online, apply it with telesales, apply it in a retail solution; all sorts of things like that. The more methods of attraction you can use, the more profitable you'll be and the more customers you'll acquire.

You don't need to master each of the following things before you can make profitable and scalable sales, but not being competent will cost you money, so here's what you need to be aware of:

You need to make sure you get the return on investment right and learn step by step in your sales and marketing approach, because without being too crude, many agencies, media owners and organisations like that will take your money and abuse your good nature and your willingness to spend money with them. You have to be really, really sharp when it comes to getting the best deal. It's something I do an awful lot for people, because it's not just about negotiating the best rate; it's about getting the best return on your investment. To be honest, when you get the mechanics right, spending £10,000 plus on something is a no-brainer because you're going to get, as we said earlier, way more than that back in profit every time you do it.

The other thing to mention here is that there is no such thing as free when it comes to advertising, marketing, PR or any promotional tool. 'Free' is a misconception because you have your time invested in it and that is not free.

People say you should do, for example, search engine optimisation (SEO). As it stands today as I write this book, search engine optimisation is not a great way to promote your business. It doesn't mean you shouldn't put the right keywords and phrases in your website or landing pages, but you should be able to spend money to attract the customers and convert that to profit. Spending money getting your SEO right costs money, it's not a free service, so don't think of anything you do in terms of attraction as free, because even if it's just your own time in doing it, that has a value, a significant value. That's relevant whether it's digital things, traditional, advertising and marketing, cross-media things, all sorts of things like that.

One of the things I love to do and I've been very successful at, particularly with big brands, is doing things where you take people from offline content, for example, in advertising or marketing in newspapers and magazines and bring them online with things like QR codes, interactive print, augmented reality, things like that.

That's a specialist area that I've developed over the years and I've spoken at events all around the world just on that subject, because it's one of the least used, least understood but easiest and lowest cost things to do when you get it right.

The other thing you need to think about is referrals, because when you get a referral from somebody, it's a really clever way to get customers. You need to orchestrate the way you get referrals from customers because those referred customers will be great prospects, great customers and on average, probably spend more with you, too.

As I said before, you need to know who your right prospects are and that way you can not only go after them, you can afford to go after them, too. Remember not everybody is a buyer. Some will never buy, some will buy now, some will buy soon, some will buy later on and some will buy never. Think about who is ready to buy right now. By 'right now', I mean in less than three months. Think about how you're going to qualify those people quickly.

Stop trying to twist people's arm. If they're not going to buy in the first three months or even less if it's relevant to you, fine; put them on what I would call a longer-term strategy of communication. That way, when they are ready to make the decision to buy, in maybe three to six months, or longer, they come to you because you are top of their mind.

Remember, lots of people are curious, not compelled to buy, so be careful with these people, because curious people aren't necessary customers, but you don't want to turn them away. At the same time, you need to make sure that you're focused on buyers who are buying now and those that would buy later but don't treat them the same.

There are too many people with no real interest in what you offer; they really have a lack of appreciation for you and what you can do for them. On the internet marketing side as an example, how many people sign up for a webinar or some free training but never actually turn up or use it? It doesn't mean they're not interested in the subject but they have more pressing things to deal with, they're not going to spend their time, money or efforts on something unless they're ready to do it, which is fine. But you don't want to lose out on that prospect later on, particularly if you paid to get that lead. Just treat them differently. Think about how you're going to treat them.

Know a prospect's motivating factors, because if they were keen enough, for example, to sign up for a webinar, at some point they're going to come back to you or come back to the subject matter and you need to know what the triggers are that will get them to do that.

Remember, you can segment prospects and focus on getting new prospects in the best segments. Take the people who have bought now and upsell to them. Take the people who haven't done what you'd like them to do and get them back in so they're close to you for when they're ready to buy.

Just think about using media correctly. Something like video can be used in multiple places nowadays with much lower cost. You can use it on TV, but you can also use it online, whether that's in places like YouTube or on your own website. But think about all sorts of media. You don't have to stick with one or just be thinking: "I can't afford to do those particular things."

You can do display advertising in local media, in national media or in international media. As I said, there's TV. You have radio. You can do interactive print as I talked about earlier. You can even do interactive second-screen TV now, which is something I've worked on quite a lot, too. There are tools like Shazam, but there's also some other very clever technologies right around the corner.

Think about the packaging and the point-of-sale material that you use if it's a physical product. In some of our businesses, we spend a vast amount of time, money and effort getting packaging and point-of-sale right.

When it comes to, for example, direct mail or advertising in magazines and newspapers, you can use what's called a PURL (personal URL). Those can be great for engagement and measurement too. Catalogues and brochures: we do serious business by using catalogue and brochures correctly. To distinguish them, catalogues are something that people can look through and order from, brochures are almost like an advertisement.

A good tip that I was told many years ago is if you're going to create a brochure for what you do, you need to structure it, so if somebody reads it from cover to cover, it's almost like a story. If you were sitting there with a prospect, you could open that brochure and talk them through your sales pitch with page-by-page turning that really educates them. Brochures need to be educational. Too many people don't do that and don't have the brochure flow the way it should.

You can use other formats of media. The phone is a great thing, whether it's a mobile or landline. Text messages are effective too. PR – press can be really powerful when you get it right. So how do you actually define what you're going to use? Obviously, you have a financial implication because although TV, if you locally advertise, is not so expensive, you may not even have that budget; so you need to manage what you're doing.

The first thing you want to be able to do is look at the market you're serving. Do some competitive and market analysis because you want to target the ideal audience. You want to deliver the best offers out there for that market. You want to be thinking about the profit and the gaps in an existing market and what you do.

You want to implement a systematic approach, where you're getting that direct response aspect to collecting leads and things like that, so you can revisit them; whether that's with retargeting adverts or retargeting through e-mail or direct mail. Look at what the market wants and at what your competitors are doing and then be innovative here too.

Remember your audience. Think about:

- Who is your ideal buyer?

- Where do they hang out, both physically and digitally?

- Who's already selling to them?

- How can you best target them?

Here's another little tactic. When you are promoting and publicising what you do, attracting new customers, as I say, keep your powder dry. Don't use your best stuff up front. What I suggest you do is what I call 'sizzle'. You allude to your best stuff. But the reason you don't want to do your best things up front, first of all, particularly if you're using a Sniper approach, is you need to have something behind you or in reserve that you can follow up with if they don't bite.

I'm not saying don't use great content, because just like a music artist who wants to sell music, they know that the money, for example, is in album sales. Turning up at a concert and merchandising, they need to present good content – in fact, sometimes the best content – up front to get you to buy the album. However, in marketing for non-music and things like that, you want something really good, really compelling to start with; but if they don't bite, you need to have something to follow it up maybe two or three times afterwards, that's even better, so when they've seen you provide this information they think: "If this is what they're giving away for free, what you pay for must be incredible."

That's the strategy I would use. Deliver great content but don't use your best content up front, because the second or third time you communicate with them and give them some education and some value, you want it to be even better. You want to build the rapport you have with them, the quality of the rapport, too, over time, because you're educating them and as they become more educated, you need to keep building on that relationship you now have.

The other thing you need to be thinking is this: not being afraid to say what your competition will not say. This is a great and unique selling proposition and shows that you're open and trustworthy. Too many people in a market hide certain things. It's better to be open, honest and admit there are market problems, issues or limiting factors because you want your prospects to actually ask the competition about something they may find awkward and question your competition's ability to look after their interests as well as you do. To be blunt, you want you prospects to feel the competition is not as trustworthy as you are.

Something else I'd like to talk about is copywriting. Copywriting is not just all about sales material, whether it be a presentation or a piece of direct mail, a letter, or a video sales letter: a presentation with words that are voiced over. I use that format quite a lot. You may even consider something known as a long form sales letter, which is a multiple-page piece of marketing or advertising that's just text.

Copy is used in everything: TV and radio ads, video, YouTube, on your website, all over the place; so you need to get competent. I'm not saying 'good', but get competent at copywriting. The best way to do that is to look at what other people are doing and what you know works and not copy it because that would be wrong; but do use it as inspiration.

However, I suggest you get really good or even excellent at writing headlines because headlines are really important. The overall look of a piece of marketing is what will stop somebody in their tracks, which is absolutely what you need to do. The headline is the next thing they're almost certain to look at, so this has to draw people in and make them want to read more.

Going back to what I said earlier about a Sniper approach or Shotgun approach, for example, if you're using a Shotgun approach in an advertisement in a magazine, you want to capture the attention of as many relevant people who are flicking through the pages as possible.

You need to design that advertisement to stop them in their tracks and then get them to read that headline and that headline needs to draw them in, it needs to intrigue them. They need to know more so they're compelled to take action. That's where direct response in a Shotgun approach with what's normally high-cost advertising can be incredibly powerful.

It's something I've done very, very well for certain brands over the years as well as for my own business.

You want to travel along what Jordan Belfort would call his 'Straight Line' sales line with your campaign. Remember we talked about a campaign rather than events. In a campaign, you are going through separate events and as you go along the campaign line with separate events, you need to be removing negatives, adding positives and changing beliefs that a buyer may have about what you provide.

You need to look at the elements in your sales and marketing funnel, what you can control and what people perceive when they go through things. That's why you need to monitor a funnel.

Let me give you another example of this. Just take video, for example. When I use video online, I host and have certain things on social media; but I prefer to use a system called Wistia. The reason I use it is that they have some very, very clever analytics on the video. You might say, as most people would: "Somebody watches the video and they take action or not", but actually, that's not the whole story. You can put a video together and through things like Wistia, not only can you see how many people have viewed it, you can also see how many people have viewed it more than once. You can see where they've stopped watching it, where they've dropped off, whether they watched all the way to the end. There are lots and lots of analytics to do with video and because you have those analytics in place, you can actually monitor what's working and what's not.

For example, in one newspaper, we did some interactive print, and what was very interesting was that the newspaper was a U.K. national weekend newspaper with millions of readers. We were able to determine not only that the readers of that newspaper preferred beer to wine, which is not really what the demographic profile of the newspaper would suggest, but also how long a video about beer or how long a video about wine they would watch.

If you're promoting and you understand the statistics, you can tailor what you deliver to an audience based on what you know they will consume. You can really trim your message or elongate your message perfectly for the target market. Remember, maths is the easiest way to control your sales and sales people, so get those metrics in place and make use of them.

As we're getting further along - because this is quite a big section - remember, your goal is to close anybody who will and should be closed because you're actually helping them. Because you should add value and help people by selling to them I have four questions and these four questions are the ones I ask before I work with people on a one-to-one level or invest in them because they show what you know and what you need to learn to make sales, so here they are:

Question 1: Do you know your customers? We've talked a bit about that before.

Question 2: How many of them do you know? If you have a thousand customers, how many of those customers do you genuinely know and genuinely understand?

Question 3: Do you know the end users of what you provide? This may or may not be relevant for you, for example, if you supply a retailer and they sell it on, do you know that end user? If you're in a service industry, you may actually be a sub-contractor so do you know who the end client is?

Question 4: How many of them do you know?

Let's imagine you are producing electric toothbrushes and you sell them en masse, wholesale to various retailers. There's a very good chance you'll know your customers and you'll know most of them. You might know some of them very well and some of them only a little bit. But how many of the people who actually use the electric toothbrush do you know? If the answer is 'not most of them', you need to change the way you're doing things so you do know the end users and get to know most of them. That's where having the right system in place to attract customers fits in. That's why it's very, very strategic and requires that ESTO approach to how you do things.

If you can get to the end users, your insight, your knowledge and your ability to not just sell to them later but to really educate your customers and the end users absolutely skyrockets. It will make a huge difference to your sales.

In reality, as with the prospects, you need to be thinking about how you simultaneously repel those who are not buyers now or never will be, as they waste your time and money. Think about who is a buyer and getting connected with them. Get connected with as many people who are relevant and who are potentially making you money as possible.

Think about, in your attraction strategies, going back to the ESTO principle; make sure you're aware that everybody who needs to know knows who you are and what they need to know, too. It's not just the questions that people ask - the frequently asked questions - there are questions that people should ask but they don't. In your strategy, you need to think about that.

You also need to think that some people get ignored and some people ignore the needs of customers or end users or whoever it is. You need to manage and change certain things in the way you promote, the way you attract customers - again through education - that doesn't ignore needs and doesn't hide things that they should and need to know.

Remember, some people want to take action but actually don't know what action they should be taking or could be taking. Help them out. You need to make sure that by educating them and providing the direct response principles as well as the branding principles, you are helping them to take the next step on the journey between becoming a prospect and actually being a customer.

What I want you to think about here is that last aspect when you have people positively taking action. What I'm going to use here is Dan Sullivan's definition of marketing from back in chapter two: it's about 'proactively doing things is good for them'. The best way to do this is by giving what are called results in advance. This is all part of the education-based strategy.

If you can give somebody a small quick win, even a small step towards where they want to be from where they are now, with the information you give them absolutely free, not only will they know you, they'll like you, they'll trust you and they'll be compelled to want more from you.

Before we finish up this chapter, however, remember we have some tasks to do. Remember too, especially for this chapter, you can get not just the tasks but the video too on the promotional strategies with marketing, advertising, PR, etc. from the website www.MoreSalesThanYouCanHandle.com.

The tasks for this chapter are:

- Identify where your ideal prospects hang out physically and digitally.

- Look at whether they're visible or hidden.

What does that mean? Visible people are people who you could get in contact with, for example, buying a mailing list or doing some targeting on Facebook advertising or something like that. Hidden people are people you don't know necessarily exist or who are more difficult to get hold of. For example, you may be looking to target people who do accountancy and you can probably buy an e-mail list, a direct mail list or any other list of people who are accountants or accountancy practices. They're quite visible.

However, the other side of the coin could be that you're out there looking for what I would call hidden people. Let's say for example that you are in the legal profession and you're looking for people who are financially struggling, who may need to go bankrupt. Those people tend not to be that visible. They're hidden. So, you need to influence those people. You need to have the right approach. Knowing if your prospects are easily contactable, visible, or fairly well hidden will influence the approach you take. You need to know: are they hidden or visible?

- You need to figure out the three to five most common questions people have about what you do and answer them.

- You need to work out what you can give them for little or no cost, that in just five or ten minutes will really help them take a step closer to their ultimate goal and that you can help them achieve as a quick win for them.

- You've heard of thinking outside the box. I don't want you to think outside the box. That's pretty boring and actually, too many people think that's a solution. It's not. You need to be looking for another box. What do I mean by that? You need to be looking at other markets, not just your own if you want to get exponential results. You do that by using the E, the Entrepreneurial side in the ESTO principles.

What I want you to do now is look at your market, but look at other markets too and think: What are they doing that's successful? How are they approaching people? What are they doing? Sign up on a few e-mail lists. Make contact with people in other industries. See how they promote, what they do, what they don't do, what they do well, what they don't do well.

Really learn and be entrepreneurial and innovate and move the game forward, move the game on in your market. Because not only thinking outside the box but looking for another box is where you'll make massive indents and massive profits, while your competitors really struggle and when you put up barriers your competitors will need to get over them, leaving you to sell and continually develop, generating more sales than you can handle.

# CHAPTER 10

## HOW TO BUILD EFFECTIVE AND PERSUASIVE RAPPORT

When compelling prospects before, during and after a sale, you have to build the right rapport with them and at the same time support your brand values, too. In this chapter, I'm going to share with you exactly how you can do this.

People buy when they love your product or service, they trust and connect with you and they trust and connect with your company, if you're representing a company. But the other thing is, as we talked about before, people get excited by the opportunities, so you need to give them some logic, as well, and we've talked about that, too.

One thing that people get wrong in many sales and marketing courses, books and information is how to close. The reality is, yes, you need that excitement, you need the opportunity, you need to help somebody along, but the more money or more resources somebody needs to put into something, the more logic you need to provide. As strange as it sounds, resources, whether that's money, time, effort or it could even be change because that's actually a resource too, the more logic you have to put in place.

The way you communicate this also has to be done correctly and the way to do it is in line with the market. But as I said before, you need to be what I would call slightly aspirational, slightly beyond the comfort zone, because that's where the greatest things happen.

You'll recall I talked about when you go into a meeting, making sure that you're dressed the right way for the audience. But you have to use things like tonality. You have to care. You have to use body language and things such as neuro-linguistic programming techniques. You have to use the right phrases. All those things are really important as you're building that connection because rapport is something that people pick up on, not just through the words, not just through the tonality and the way you say things, but through every piece of communication they're exposed to.

Think about the senses – there's sight, there's sound, there's smell, there's touch. All of these things are absolutely relevant in building rapport. For example, if you're in a situation where you're talking with somebody and they're trying to explain to you what you need to do to move forward because of a problem you may have, but they smell and they don't smell in a good way, it is not going to help build rapport.

Although in theory how somebody smells is going to have very little impact on what you think a sales marketing process will be, actually it has a massive impact. In the other way, if you have way too much perfume or aftershave on, that's not good either. You need to think about really subtle things, and the most sophisticated people, when it comes to sales, marketing and customer service, use all the senses.

You go into retail stores now and they actually have certain aromas in the store because they know that this actually encourage you to buy. Did you know, if people are looking around a house they're interested in buying, if they can smell fresh bread, that's a positive thing; it makes people feel homely. Baking doesn't sell you a house, multiple factors do, but it can certainly help.

On top of that, I always recommend that you need to actually develop what I would call a big idea in order to stand out. A big idea doesn't need to be big as in grand or big as in a real enormity to grasp hold of; it can be a big idea but just a small part of the solution. That way, it's completely imaginable. People can really associate with it and that will help you immensely.

Let me give you an example. It might well be, for example, you sell property and you have a particular idea about the way you're going to manage home viewings. I'm certainly not in that industry, but I know that when I've looked to buy a property or sell a property, I'm highly disappointed with agents and particularly on the rentals, which I do quite a lot of as a property owner; it's quite frustrating sometimes.

Your big idea could just be the way you provide customer service and the attention to detail is way beyond what other people are doing. It doesn't mean you need to revolutionise the whole situation, just a small part, but a small part that's meaningful. It's a big idea that somebody can latch onto and think: "You know what? I really associate with that. That's what I'm looking for."

At the same time, if you can present your big idea by removing limiting beliefs people have and the prospect's a qualified buyer, because they want the solution and can afford it and you've worked on that through education, you all of a sudden put yourself in a position of strength. However, you also put yourself in a position where because you're removing limiting beliefs, you have that big idea and you have the right communication strategy; you're building rapport almost on a compound level, something that's incredibly powerful in the sales marketing process.

I want you to start thinking about presenting a solution where you're sorting out mental clutter in your prospect's mind, a physical mess or simplifying things for your ideal buyer. The clearer you make it for somebody, the more clutter and mess you can remove from what you're proposing and the easier it is for somebody to see through the clutter that they're currently in and to see how they don't need to be in that, the better your positioning will be and the better rapport you will build, because part of rapport is not stressing people out.

When you start simplifying things, even if it's with small building blocks in the way you do things and your education-based approach of things, you almost automatically eliminate overwhelm, stress, tension and consequently remove so many barriers to making a sale that it's the most effective way to build rapport and make the sale.

People want a level of certainty and they want what I call significance, as well. They want to feel valued and want people to see that value. But here's the thing: we as human beings also like a level of uncertainty and if your solution, whether it's a product or a service, doesn't have some uncertainty in it, you'll also struggle with it. Now, I know that's almost counterintuitive, but here's the thing: you want to put uncertainty into a sales and marketing proposition, wherever you can, in a positive way.

For example, you could say that by approaching something in this way and buying this new piece of machinery, you could, at a bare minimum, increase your productivity as a business by 18%. But you can then say: "However, that's just the start; you could go far further than that if you do certain things." You are putting positive uncertainty into a pitch and that will get, as I would say, the juices flowing; getting people really excited by your solution and how they can take what is certain and build on it.

Think about how you can use uncertainty, where most people see it as a negative, as a really positive thing. Also, you need to be saying: "The scale of the result is guaranteed at a minimum." By having that, you have guarantees in place that give a level of confidence and certainty to an existing situation that they can completely understand.

I want you to start thinking through what I call "big picture" questions and these need to be based on future results. A big picture, an overall view, is for example, once you have something in place, once you've bought into a product or a service that's on offer: "Here's what the big picture will look like." A really positive thing with a level of certainty, a level of significance so people can see that they're really making ways of achieving things but also there's some room for growth and uncertainty there, too.

You want to get prospects to visualise that big picture and then start to drill down. How do you do that? You first of all want to drill down to find out exactly what the buying mechanisms or the reasons for buying are. Too many people assume that, for example, the price is the issue that's preventing a sale and actually, you may find that it's not price at all; it might be their knowledge of you, their knowledge of your company, their knowledge of what's possible. Actually, it could be that what you're selling is almost too inexpensive for them to think it will be realistically doing what you promised.

There are lots of things here, but you can start to drill down. The way to drill down is to ask things, but make sure when you're asking, you don't ask invasive questions or things that are potentially embarrassing, because this puts people's guard up. For example, if I'm talking with a sales force and I want to gather information: I've given them a big picture, I've given them some questions. For example: "What would your sales results be like if you did something that I proposed?" I can get them to talk about: "I could increase my sales by 50%. I could do certain things. I wouldn't have to do all the things I don't like, for example cold calling and that sort of thing." But then saying: "What things do you do wrong in a sales call?" That's quite an invasive thing. It's quite negative. It's potentially quite embarrassing, particularly because people don't like to admit defeat or admit failure. You could also find situations where you can ask: "Why didn't you make money after that situation?"

Don't attack people. Don't be invasive. Don't ask things that could embarrass somebody. You can actually re-word things so they are positive. Instead of talking about specific things that are negative, you could talk about general things. You could use words like 'approximately' or 'in a roundabout way'. That way, people don't feel you're attacking them on specific items and that's really positive for starting to drill down and to build rapport.

You want to get people to talk. Actually, as long as they're talking on a specific topic that suits you, you want to keep them talking and let them talk, because remember, their favourite subject is themselves and you can learn as you're going through and tailor your pitch as they go through, solving problems by listening.

At the end of the day, your goal is to find out what your client's - what I would call – 'Why' is. Why will they do something and why won't they do something? So you need to be able to think about questions that you can use in all sorts of situations.

I highly recommend that you actually memorise perfect questions for situations and industries and have them almost at the tip of your tongue as and when you hear a prospect say something that relates to that question. Then you can start to move from general situations to specific situations.

As I said earlier, by being the question master, you have authority in a situation. The way to really build on this authority of question asking is not by asking them permission to ask questions but by stating that you're going to do something to help them.

For example, you don't say: "Would you mind if I ask you a couple of quick questions?" You say, "Just a couple of quick questions. I don't want to waste your time and I want to help you," or "Just a couple of quick questions so I can better help you." Those are positive things. I haven't asked for permission, I've used tonality and I've been there to help them and the question is helpful but not invasive. It's not aggressive; it's a positive thing.

How do you then tailor that to what you specifically do? If you're selling a product or a service they've used before, I highly recommend that you use questioning to find out what people like or dislike about what they've done in the past. When people have prior experience and feel they're experts in a particular situation, particularly their own personal situation; that can be dangerous in a sales context, so you want to find out what they liked and disliked and associate accordingly with what you do and don't do.

People also pay more for something customised to them and for something that's new and innovative, so you need to think about what people have used before, where you fit in and how you can customise what you do and be innovative for them, because that will get you more money for what you do.

You also need to think about how you could change or improve what you currently have to suit them or to suit the market moving forward. Going back to my ESTO principles, it's the Entrepreneurial side. Think about what you can change and improve over time to move the game on.

You want to know what the prospect's biggest headache is. You want to know what their ultimate objective is. You also need to have an idea of a program or methodology that you can clearly explain to them, that's really working for you as a business, but also works for them, so you can find out if that fits with what they do.

I've been in many situations where I've made a suggestion to somebody and the reason they haven't taken me up on the situation that I'm proposing is they don't feel that the program I'm offering is something they can integrate into the way they do business. This happens for many reasons, primarily because people are adversely affected by change, or so they believe. Again, that's a limiting belief.

But if you know how they do something and you can fit in with that great. If you need to propose something that suits that way you work and you know would work for them, you have be able to clearly define why they should be doing this, why it's much better, much easier for them and will get them the results, particularly if they're already in that marketplace. You have to work out what factors are most important to them.

Something you can ask, for example, at the end of a conversation, may be: "Have I asked every detail that's important to you?" That way you're actually opening up and saying: "Is there anything else you should tell me?"

Remember, you let people talk. Don't interrupt people with solutions. This is a major failure of many sales situations and sales people. Remember, I talked about keeping your powder dry? Let people talk, let them feel a bit of pain; let them visualise what they could be doing.

Actually, one other mistake people make is almost talking themselves out of the sale. When somebody is ready to commit, they're compelled to buy, it's amazing how many salespeople keep talking. Actually, there's a point at which a good salesperson recognises that the close is automatic and actually, a continued conversation and a continued sales pitch will deter them from giving the money. That's something to work on, too.

Remember, if somebody's in a painful situation, its okay to let them feel a little bit of their pain; but don't over state or develop that pain too much because you don't want to be associated with it when building that rapport with them. You want to really sympathise and empathise with them, and then say: "Yes, I totally understand your pain," or "I can really appreciate and associate with you on that. However, do you know that it's not difficult to change that situation?" You build rapport based on positive things and moving people from where they are now to where you want to take them and where they want to be.

Remember, don't try and push people to take action in sales; think about taking action in areas other than just buying. I've seen that happen before, because when you have to run through a set of stages between a prospect starting out and a prospect being a customer, rushing them is a major issue and something that does not build rapport. Think about the prospect's belief system and how they need to work and their emotional wants and needs, which could be the amount of time they need to go and evaluate things.

Remember, I talked before about when you're in a situation, whether it's a face-to-face meeting, a phone call, or even something at distance; an advertisement or piece of direct mail, give them something to do. Give them some work to go and think through and handle before they come back to you, because that builds rapport. Again, it builds your position of authority.

If they shift away from providing things that you've asked them for, you can then direct them back or make the decision that these are not your best buyers. Walking away is a good way of building rapport, too.

Remember, questions can be leading in a good way. For example you could ask: "How long have you been thinking about doing something?" You're assuming and putting into their mind the assumption that they are thinking about it and if they're not currently thinking about it, particularly if it's solving a problem they have, it will really engage them quickly.

If they have been thinking they have a problem or they need to take advantage of an opportunity, saying: "How long have you been thinking about it?" or saying to them you understand their situation and you want to take them out of the problem or give them the opportunity, when they think to themselves, "I've been thinking about this for quite a while," that puts in an element of pain and motivation in place. So use leading questions where you can in the positive way.

One last thing on this section before we get to the task: try and build and associate with other people on what I would call common grounds. For example, it might be friends, religions, sports. You need to find some real, honest common ground; don't just agree with them if you personally don't because not only is that untrue but you'll get found out and that's not a good way to build rapport.

In virtually every situation, if you find out that somebody, for example, does a particular type of sport that you've never done in your life and you probably don't think about all that often, for example, archery, something very different, not the normal type of sporting activity, one thing you could say to somebody is: "Yes, that sounds really interesting. It's something I'd love to have to go out one time or another." you then build a rapport with them even though you've never done archery in your life. If you're honest with somebody and you're enthusiastic about what they are doing or what they like, that is a perfect way to build rapport.

On that basis, let's talk about the task. Remember, you'll find this and more information at MoreSalesThanYouCanHandle.com. There's just one thing this time because last time you had an awful lot to do, but don't forget: you're building every single time.

This time, I want you to write out a rapport-building script that you can almost learn and recite off by heart and have it at hand with the perfect questions that you could use in a sales situation based on your market sector. Remember, you're looking to serve the customers, serve the prospects.

If you remember, last time, we talked about education-based quick wins. I want you to build a script, I want you to learn it, I want you to have some questions around it, that as you're listening to your prospects, you can throw into the conversation or you can use at a later date with your campaigns for marketing. Questions that really help people and draw in what you learned in the last chapter and this chapter to build amazing rapport.

# CHAPTER 11

## BE THE QUESTION MASTER

There are many ways people try to control a situation and build rapport. But one - if not the most powerful - way in a sales and marketing situation, is to ask questions. We briefly touched on that in the last chapter.

Not only are questions a great way to learn from your prospects and customers, they're also a way to direct and control the conversation, as the person asking the question is in a leadership position. It's also impossible, based on the way our brains work, not to try to answer a question. This is why, in this chapter, I want to take you further into questioning so that you can learn exactly what you need to know to become a question master.

Now, as I mentioned, people's number one subject is themselves. This is the key to building trust. Questions are not just a great way to listen, but they're also a great way to learn at the same time. You can use questions to build emotion for what you do, support the beliefs you're looking to create and cement logic in taking action.

The way people actually behave is based on visual, auditory and kinaesthetic triggers. You can add olfactory into there as well, which is taste. But what you fundamentally have is visual, so seeing things, auditory, which is listening to things, and kinaesthetic, which is feeling things.

We all have a bias towards one of them, although the others play their part too; but what you need to do when you're asking questions or when you're giving information is utilise these influencing factors by asking questions in a certain way; then you can start to see what people respond to most. We'll talk about that a little bit later, in presentation styles, but it's a key skill that can radically improve your results.

The tactic when questioning people is to have them make up their own mind. This will be a combination of, maybe, feeling pain and visualising better things. You want things to be bigger, brighter, better, more intense in the future in a positive way. You want to get people into that idea of feeling pain or feeling frustration and then visualising the improvements; that's the way you ask questions. You don't want to do things in an over-simplistic way here. Yes, you can ask really easy questions, but just like a good interviewer on TV or radio, you don't want to ask questions where people can give you small, short answers like yes or no. You need prospects to be able to answer the question fully and get emotionally involved in what they're doing.

Remember, you need to be using questions to get people to think about what's called future pacing – their future. You need to make assumptions and similar aspects, which are a part of neuro-linguistic programming. When you have those in place and you understand that there are visual, auditory and kinaesthetic triggers, you can start to use questions in a slightly different way.

If, for example, you were in a restaurant and you were looking to find out about somebody, you could say to them: "What do you think looks good on the menu?" That is a visual question. You could change that question to: "What do you think sounds good on the menu?" That's an auditory question. You can then go to kinaesthetic by saying: "What do you think would taste nice on the menu?" That's more a feeling way to ask the question.

That is a very simple example of the same question asked in three different ways. I highly recommend that the key questions you're going to use, you build in different ways of asking; with visual, auditory or kinaesthetic triggers, or alternatively and particularly useful in a group situation where you're talking to multiple people, being able to involve all those things together.

For our menu example you could ask: "What on the menu looks or sounds nice and do you think will taste good?" That gets all three of those things in. It doesn't matter which of those three is your dominant factor; we've encouraged you to use that and involved you more personally than just using one way of asking.

I want you to start using proven questioning techniques and also start making assumptions in your questions. I said earlier about assuming things based on neuro-linguistic programming. For example, you could start by saying to people: "After you've started making money, what would you do next?" You've automatically said to them and made them assume that by doing what you're suggesting, you are making money. There's no question there that you might not make money. You've assumed they will. It's this future pacing in a positive way.

Know your questions; tailor them to future pacing. Tailor them to auditory, visual, kinaesthetic triggers and make sure that you're not asking a question somebody's already answered, either, because they want to believe that you are always listening to them. Remember they're the most important person in their own world.

People say to me: "The world doesn't revolve around you." Actually my world does revolve around me because it's how I see things: you need to remember that when you're in a sales and marketing situation.

Think about what you need to use in terms of tonality, in terms of the way you respond. If you've answered a question and somebody's responded to you, just like a good interviewer on the TV, they'll nod, they'll actually confirm things and they'll give that person a feeling of confidence, that I call significance. That's really key to being a great question master.

Use your facial expressions and body language to add to the building of rapport. You want to be able to say and get people to understand, even without words, that you care. You also want to be saying things, as I mentioned last time, such as: "I'm just like you." That's a great way to use questioning and to build rapport. These two things alone will make you highly successful in sales and marketing, as strange and simplistic as that sounds.

But here's another thing. The greatest skill of all is enthusiasm, but don't confuse enthusiasm for pressure. You want to be there and enthusiastic for somebody but not force them into a situation. Remember, you're coming at it from their perspective.

Other things you can do to help are what's called match and mirror somebody. You want to be using the same movements as them. I'm not going to go into lots of things on matching and mirroring and neuro-linguistic programming because that's not what this book is about, but I would highly recommend that you start to learn a little bit about those things.

When you can connect with somebody on an emotional and physical level, and then throw questions in too, it's really excellent for building rapport and compelling people to buy.

Let's also think about words you can use in a question context. When somebody's answering your question, use words like: "That's great," "That's perfect," or "That's absolutely ideal." You also want to say things like: "It's good to know that." You can use a little bit of positive inflection in your voice to build them up.

Don't think to yourself about removing their pain completely, however.

For example, if somebody is in a situation where it's not good and they're talking and they're saying: "Things are really difficult at the moment, I'm struggling to work out what to do next," you don't say to them anything that removes their pain. What you do is you respond to them as they're talking by saying something like: "I totally understand." With the right tonality, it shows you care. That's actually part of being a good question master.

Remember, you need to think about what things people could take offence to or put their guard up around. You want to talk about things like money or a financial situation in particular in quite a disarming tone. You need to be relaxed and non-threatening. People who are threatened are not going to become your customers.

Think to yourself: how can you build rapport through questions? How can you listen to questions and respond so as to improve your position within that relationship, build that rapport, position yourself as the expert, position yourself as the helpful person?

You also need to think that, because time is money, you need to not spend too much time in certain question areas. You're going to have to go through the process, but equally, you need to use your questions and your ability to respond to those questions to keep people moving towards where you want to get to; not rushing them, but not letting them go off on a tangent or somewhere that's not going to help you.

We talked earlier about having a big picture, a big idea. You need to get the emotion, the logic in place so people become qualified and are ready to buy. The way you then use questions and close a situation - because remember, at the right point, they're compelled to want to buy from you - comes down to this one thing, and its simplicity is its power. All you need to do is say something in a question like: "Does this idea make sense to you?" or "Do you see the true beauty of what we're talking about here?"

Get them to agree. Get them to realise that it's no big deal. You're asking a question and if they don't agree with you, they've got the ability, without feeling threatened, to say: "No, I don't agree."

So if you say: "Does the idea make sense to you?" It's no big deal. But if somebody says: "No, not really," your next question can be: "Why is that the case?" You've listened to them, you've responded in a positive way and you're overcoming objections. If they say no or delay, that's okay, and it's right. But don't worry. It's best not to rush somebody. Just find out what the sticking points are and deal with them.

This is the best way to use questions and tell people the benefits you have to offer, getting them through any problems that they face so that they take action; they actually take positive action that is beneficial for them.

The last thing I want to say when it comes to questions, before we get to the task, is you need to be thinking about how you structure your questions so that people will do things because they feel they are going to lose out if they don't.

I'll give you a story in a moment, but people, no matter what they think or what they want to do, will work harder to keep what they have and not miss out than to actually get new things. Prospects don't want to waste what they have now and don't want to lose out. Bad things happening or loss of something is the bigger motivation here.

You need to be asking a question or doing something so that people don't actually think to themselves: "I'm not sure I want to do that". They've got to be thinking: "If I don't do that, I'm missing out."

Here's a personal example from when I was very young. I was at a swimming pool with my family. My grandfather was there. Quite honestly, the swimming pool was freezing cold. I was only about five or six years old, but I remember it to this day.

I was not interested in going swimming, even though I absolutely loved swimming. The pool was just too cold. My parents tried everything. However, my grandfather was very clever when it came to this. He was actually a magician and he really understood how to ask people questions and how to get them to do things; that's literally part of a magician's bag of tricks. He came over to me. I was sat on the side. He said: "Do you not want to come here later?"

I thought to myself, without hesitation: "I don't want to miss out."

Then he followed this up by saying: "If you don't get into this swimming pool now, you will not come back later."

You would not believe how quickly I jumped into that swimming pool. What happened is he asked me a leading question, knowingly or not knowingly, about me losing out on something in the future and he then made a statement that said: "You must do this, otherwise, you will miss out."

That is what people almost always take action on. Think about that in the way you question things and the actions you ask people to take after a question.

Now, on to the task here. What I want you to do is, first of all, head over to MoreSalesThanYouCanHandle.com. You'll find the information for this task there.

I want you to write at least five questions that you can use that can be done visually, auditorially or kinaesthetically as phrases, or five questions in which you can link all three together that will get you from your starting point with a prospect to where you need to make a sale.

Then, think about the answers you expect somebody to give to each of those questions, so you've got a response to them all, so you're 100% prepared or at least as prepared as you ever could be, no matter what happens, as you are several steps ahead of your prospects in the sales conversation. And remember, over time, you're going to refine that, but you need to have a starting point – it's as simple as that.

# CHAPTER 12

# HOW TO MAKE A POWERFUL PRESENTATION

I've talked in the previous chapters about building rapport and asking questions, but the reality is, when it comes to sales and marketing, you're going to have to do some presentations. It doesn't matter whether that's in person, on video, on the phone, through advertisements, through direct mail or on social-media channels; no matter what it is, you need to think about presenting information in the right way.

In this chapter, that's what I want to do for you. I want to give you the right tools, techniques and material, so no matter what you do, you can tailor a presentation across any media channel to get the best results.

Make sure, first of all, your presentation and visuals are professional. There are too many people who create unprofessional things. It's not expensive to do presentations correctly. But equally, you tend to see people over-complicate them.

By being professional, you want to make sure to remember we're talking about direct response techniques and branding techniques. If you over design them, over complicate them and make them difficult to follow, you actually reduce the chance of success.

As human beings, we retain information in various ways. If we just see something, we retain about 20% of it. If we hear something, we retain about 20% of it, too. If you're doing a presentation and you have the chance to visually talk through something, you should do that. Personally it's difficult for me to tell you that, because I hate doing things like PowerPoint presentations; I feel my subject is better talked through as a discussion, but I appreciate and I do actually have visual aids for what I do, whether it's a PowerPoint, print outs or anything else; because the priority is the prospect, not me. I understand, even though it's not what I'd like to do, that I have to do things so people see and hear because it's better for communication.

When you do use audio and visual together, you actually give people the opportunity to retain 50% of the information, which is far better than the 20% when you just see something or 20% when you just hear. You've more than doubled the retention level of your audience, so it's a 'no brainer'.

However, you also need to think about how we do things. 85% of the information that we take in is through our eyes. 80% of motivation is actually optically stimulated, too. Remember, you need to think about these things all the time and I'm going to tell you more about that later.

When you're in a sales and marketing situation, getting somebody involved straightaway is really beneficial, simply because on day one the prospect is actually a pretty hot prospect. But the down side is that over time, they're going to cool off. In simple terms, by day three or four, if you've not really connected with them, they've probably forgotten your name and that's particularly relevant when you're distance selling. You need to be thinking about how you continue a conversation, even if it's by e-mail or phone, so as to stay top of a prospect's mind.

Remember going back to creating a campaign, not just an event and the follow up and how you deal with things with maybe seven to 20 communications or instances where they see you before they take action? That's really critical here; so you need to be thinking about what materials you're sending to people and how they can see, hear and feel what you're about. That will keep them maybe not hot, as a prospect, but at least warm.

Human beings, through our eyes, can deal with about 1.5 million elements in a single image simultaneously; our brains are fantastic at filtering out things that they don't need to focus on. We can also, believe it or not, comprehend words about five times faster than we actually speak, which is somewhere in the region of 150 words per minute. So, if for example, you were doing something on a radio station with an advert, you can increase the speed at which you talk in that advertisement and get more information shared in the time available. It will reduce your costs but you can actually still comprehend what people are saying. It doesn't reduce your ability to connect with somebody.

Visual aids give the ability to tell probably 40% more story in the same time and as I said earlier, will improve the audience's actual recognition and their ability to retain information. It also, at the same time, raises audience expectation. That's something that you really want to think about.

But here's the thing. This is what I tend to do, because it's all very well showing somebody something and talking them through it, but because your eyes can take in 1.5 million images simultaneously and because in life there are so many distractions nowadays, people sit and watch the TV and while the TV's on they may be talking to other people, they may be on their phone or tablet, multitasking, they may have things going on outside that take their attention away from what you want to present. Those are all risks; so what you do is use the visual aids; the auditory, visual and kinaesthetic tools I've talked about earlier, but then when you want them to really focus, get them to do something with you, a task, just as I'm doing in this book with tasks at the end. As soon as you ask somebody to do something, their focus has to shift. It doesn't need to be anything big. It just needs to be something small but meaningful.

I've set some rules out. You need to be thinking, when you're doing a presentation, about telling them what you're going to tell them first. You then tell them. Then you tell them what you told them and give them something to do.

Now this is quite a simple prospect to work on with any presentation. I've actually used that to an extent in each chapter of this book. You need to be thinking about how you communicate with people through sound, through vision, through emotion, so people are thinking and going through things because that is really important to the adoption of what you're talking about, the adoption of what you're suggesting.

You want to be seen as smarter, more comprehensive; as having a better appreciation of their situation and being more thorough than anybody else. That is achieved by telling the people what you're going to tell them, telling them, and then reminding them what you've told them and giving them a task to do.

What if, for example, you were presenting and you were using something like PowerPoint? The other thing here is not to over complicate things. Keep things easy to consume and don't make them overwhelming. In PowerPoint, for example, just have one main message per page. But keep momentum up: people get bored. The number of times I've watched people present and as they're presenting, while they're really enthusiastic and involved in the subject, some of the audience begin playing with their phones, doodling on paper or checking e-mail. That, for you, is a real problem! You have not engaged your audience. You have not got them thinking about the things you want them to think about and got them involved. Remember, getting somebody to do something, giving them a task, asking them questions; these are the things that will properly engage your audience.

Again, I'll give an example. If you're actually using PowerPoint, you don't want to only have slides, you want to educate in the slides and you have to have that wow factor, because it really elevates your standing.

You need to have stories in your presentation. Stories increase recall by about 26%. You also need to use your own stories or client success stories if you can. You need to make sure your story has a point. You want to unfold and uncover a story; keep people curious and allude to upcoming information, This is what some copywriters call opening loops . As soon as you have what they call an open loop, you've hinted at something, but you don't continue enough to close that thing off.

For example, you start by saying: "I was once in the situation where a person just like you was in a really difficult predicament; they didn't know what to do. But the great thing was by following what I'm about to show you now, they managed to sort themselves out and really accomplish everything they wanted. But before I get to that…"

You've opened a loop without closing it. You've kept their interest.

People who do this really well will have an audience come and say: "Yes, but you haven't answered the question. You haven't told me what happened to that person. You haven't told me the story. You haven't finished the story off."

That's why great stories or great films have a beginning, middle and an end. Doing things well is all about opening and closing loops in the right way.

Remember you're focusing on your audience, not yourself. You need to be confident in building that rapport with people through questions, through the way you present, without being obnoxious. You need to be approachable. You need to be one of them. They need to associate with you. When you're doing that, 93% of communication is through things other than words. Make sure, even if you're just on the phone, you are presenting yourself in the right way. Make sure you're acting the right way.

As you maybe record something on a video or an audio file, you'll find that if you move your hands and you gesture, what you do will be more in tune with the audience. It's just a natural ability we have to use physicality as part of our communication, not just words and tonality.

Remember, we're looking to control a situation in sales and another great way to control, for example, a meeting, is to give people things to do physically. It actually gets them motivated, it gets their blood pumping, but it also asserts your authority. Believe it or not, people want you to be in charge. They don't want to be in a situation where if they want to take action, you are aloof or you're not actually helping them move from where they are now to where they want to be.

Physical barriers can get in the way too, like a desk. People seem to think sitting behind a desk, or having a meeting arranged in that way, puts them in a position of authority. They're absolutely right; it does. However, you're smarter than that and can change the dynamic physically of a situation by getting people, yourself included, to just stand up or move position.

For example, if you stand up in a presentation, somebody will pay you more attention; the scientists actually reckon about 26% more attention. If you're using a projector or a big screen rather than your laptop to do presentations, the size and the physicality of it has a greater impact.

Being able to put humour into what you do makes things seven times more effective when it comes to generating an interest level from your prospects. You need to also make sure that when you are presenting, no matter where you're presenting, what media channel, whether it's in person or at a distance, you have two specific types of presentation.

Number one is an elevator pitch; something very short and sweet that gets somebody interested within 20 seconds. You also, in my experience, need what I would call a ten-minute type talk. If you've ever seen the TED Talks, they are geared around a ten-minute scenario where people can impart really powerful information. If you're not experienced with TED Talks, I highly recommend you go onto YouTube and look some of them up, because there are some really incredible ten-minute talks out there.

What makes an incredible ten-minute talk is not just the knowledge and the passion of the person who is actually doing it; it's their ability to spend two or three minutes at the start on an introduction where they draw the audience in and control the situation by being the expert. They use almost a bit of an elevator pitch. Remember, they're also saying what they're going to say. They're going to tell you this, but before they get to that point, they're just sizzling; they're just alluding to what's going to happen. They're opening a loop. They're telling people what they're about to discover.

It's really a case of saying, in context: "I was once lost, then I discovered something, now it's all good." It's almost getting that emotional connection with the audience. Then they get into the meat of what they do in that ten minutes, which is all about a case study, a story or a scenario and taking a few of the ideas and expanding on them.

Then they use the last two or three minutes really to wrap up. They take the number one point or the number one takeaway without over-complicating it and reposition it to the person, telling them what they've told them and then they tell them what to do next, what action to take, which is all part of direct response principles.

Based on all that, I have a task for you. Again, head over to the website MoreSalesThanYouCanHandle.com and there will be some information there for you.

What I want you to do is look at all the presentations you have and use and refine them based on what you know now. Make sure you've got an elevator pitch and a TED-type ten-minute talk, because that will be really helpful to you.

Secondly, think about how else you can present – the formats and the media. At the moment, if, for example, you take a PowerPoint presentation out and you go through it with people, think about how you can modify that and convert it into an online video; how you can take that and make a telesales pitch.

Think about the format and the media that you use, because as I said very early on in this course, the more media outlets and the more ways you have, not only to attract people, but to make sales, the more successful you will be.

# CHAPTER 13

## MAKING THE SALE

As we've talked all the way through in this book about sales, obviously, closing is the logical, mutually beneficial conclusion to the situation. That's what we're going to cover in this chapter, because when done correctly, it's the natural conclusion and a really good thing for both parties. I want to show you exactly how we're going to do this and do it in such a way that you don't at all feel threatening or feel intimidated by asking for the sale.

Obviously, as we've talked here, you're going to believe - and rightly so - because you have a great product or service, that what you have is right for the prospect. You should actually be – as I would say - closing quite hard but not unpleasantly, because you know it's the right thing to do. But the other thing is that you need to make it really, really easy for people to give you money or take action.

There are too many times I've tried to buy something and - I almost call it an order prevention system is in place - people make it very difficult for me to give them money. That's because they keep trying to sell when I'm ready to buy, or are not listening for the buying signals. Imagine you're in a crowded bar and there's not enough bar staff, or too few people at a checkout where you want to spend money - people don't like to stand in line. Other situations occur when prospects can't communicate properly via an online web form, so ordering is not easy, or salespeople are ill-informed and don't have the material to hand and so can't help. I personally experienced, just a few days ago, a car dealer who I wanted to buy from and I had to say point blank I wanted to buy; to hand over my money for something that's not yet launched. They were that blind to my willingness to buy.

There are so many ways that people make it difficult for others to spend money with them, so I want you to think about how you take people's money and how you can make it really easy and also non-threatening, because that, believe it or not, will more than likely improve your sales by 10%, maybe even 20%, overnight, without changing anything else.

What you need to be thinking about here is what you're doing, not just during that point where you take somebody's money, but straight after. We've talked about before, during and after a sale and this is where it becomes really important.

When you get to the close, you want to offer a great guarantee, because that shows confidence in what you do. You can actually use that guarantee as part of your sales pitch, because if you're prepared to give somebody something for a period of time for nothing, or for example, you say, "There's a 30-day guarantee/no-questions-asked refund policy," that shows you have confidence in what you offer, and that's positive and part of the sales pitch.

But you have to make sure that people understand that, and it's part of your close, because closing is about making sure the prospect knows you're empathetic to their point of view and that you're there to help, that you're there to build a long-term relationship and that you're looking for people to say to you, "You did a great job. Can I please introduce you to other people I know who could also benefit?" That's what you're looking for in the close.

Remember, think about setting up a system where you're not desperate to close right now; you can wait and you should wait if it's the right thing to do. Remember, lifetime value is important here, not just the single close.

I also said earlier on in the book that you need to have multiple ways for people to say yes. This is not just the way they can give you money, whether it's online, through a phone call, in person, in a retail environment or whatever. Also don't pin all your hopes on one flagship product all the time. Sometimes people want to take a smaller step, sometimes people want the expensive VIP experience and so let them spend what they want to spend.

From my own personal point of view, if I'm given the option of the basic package or the VIP package, I'm probably going to want to buy the most expensive, because I'm programmed, just like virtually everybody out there, to assume, rightly or wrongly, that the more money I spend the better the experience will be: and I want the best.

Another thing to think about is a low trial price point or something like that where people who are more risk-averse don't feel that they're being pushed or taking big risks. You want to give them a sure-fire safe bet, because that is a really good way to close, but only if you know what you do is great and also only if you haven't closed on your preferred option. That needs to be the first thing that you do.

Think about what you want to sell and if there's resistance, put in an alternative that's less risky, less costly or more suited to that individual, which is why as you ask questions and learn about them; then you can start to use your bag of tricks to work out what they want, what their issues or goals are and how you can prescribe a solution in the advice you give to tell them what they need to do; that way, you can really turn people from prospects into customers without a problem.

One of the best ways in the consultative close is to talk through a situation with somebody, get an idea of what they're looking to do, then use your expertise to prescribe a solution. You don't need to give them all the details; you might just say, "Let me just summarise…"

You could say to somebody, for example, "My understanding is that you want to double your income, you want to increase your sales and you want to lower the number of hours you work. We could actually double your sales by using email marketing, or going out to people in a retail store and having a different selection of products so that they could up-sell and cross-sell." Give them ideas of what they could do. You're not going to give them the intricate details of how they're going to do that, but you can tell them how what you do can make the things that they want happen and the simple close at the end of that sort of conversation is literally: "Would you like me to help you do that?" You ask them the question. We're going back to being that question-master!

If you've worked with them, and you've built a solution together, predominantly with them feeling that they've made the decisions and taken the action all the way through, the chances are they are going to say: "Yes, you've helped me, you've educated me. You've shown me an opportunity; you've shown me how I can remove the problems. Of course, I'd like you to help that happen. You've already proved your value; you're already proving you can do it. I want to have you do it with me."

Remember, if you don't close, don't take it badly; learn from it and modify your pitch and your process. See it as a positive, but don't repeat mistakes. It's a common issue I see salespeople make; they repeat the same mistake over and over again and they don't modify what they do.

Sales and marketing is all about continual refinement. That's why, with the ESTO principles, you're looking at Entrepreneurship, you're looking at Strategy, you're looking at Tactics and Tools and Techniques and you're looking at Operations. They're all different, but you need to be constantly improving all of them.

Think about how you're going to deal with people post-sale or post meetings and engagements: follow-up makes a significant difference to people, even when they've given you money. Think about the fact that people cool off pretty fast. We talked about the scenario where on day one, they're a hot prospect, but on day two and three, they're not so hot. People have short memories, so you need to make sure that when they've agreed to do something your follow-up is really strong, really quick and really embraces and supports and even congratulates them on taking that step.

Too many people say, "Great," they take the order, and then nothing happens; there's no follow-up. You need to be fast. You need to support the decision. You need to use things such as customer relationship management systems correctly to continually build trust and continually build influence that gives you control and means that you control the situation for lifetime value, not just a one-off situation.

But remember, don't leave anything to chance. Become part of your client's life. Following up should be positive, not just educational, so think about how you can entertain as well as educate, because that, too, is a great follow-up strategy.

So, feel free to find out what the competition in your market do in terms of following up. If I'm going to go into a market, one of the first things I do is not just look at what the competition do, I buy into what they do and see what they do well and what they don't do well; you need to find out what the competition do and then better it. It's part of the entrepreneurial approach I like to take.

You should be giving so much value that the client should actually be saying thank you and saying, "Thanks very much for your time." You should never be in a situation where you're thanking a customer for their time; it should be the other way around. They should be lucky to have you there and know that your time is valuable, not just theirs.

So now we come to the task. Again, head over to MoreSalesThanYouCanHandle.com and there will be some things there for you to do. This is a very simple task, but really important.

I want you to list what you do currently at the point of sale and post-sale to see how you can improve it and also generate repeat business, up-sales, cross-sales and referrals, because that is the way to maximise your success, maximise your profit and build a lifestyle and a lifetime value that both you and your customers really appreciate.

# CHAPTER 14

## BRINGING IT ALL TOGETHER

We're now right at the end of the book and I want to bring everything together in one place. That will be a great resource for you to refer back to at a later date, because there's been so much information in this book.

If I were teaching it to you in person, it would probably be several weeks' worth of working with you and trying to perfect everything; but in a book, we can't do that. However, in this chapter I want to do my best to bring it all together, simplify it down and give you the steps on which you need to be focussed to really radically and exponentially get the results you want over time, over and over again; just in case we never get to work together.

First of all, everything is based on the customer. You can charge more and will have more clients when you have the disciplines in place, the confidence and the patience not to chase after the wrong type of prospects and the Entrepreneurial side: the Strategy, the Tactics, Techniques and Tools and the Operational procedures and people in place to deliver your products and services.

Remember, you want to be working on a core story and a pitch to massive groups of people. You need your elevator pitch and your ten-minute TED-type talk. You need to be thinking about a best buyer strategy, because it's the least expensive way to double or more your success.

Best customers are potentially not just good because of who they are: they pay the bill on time, they don't moan about what they do, they see money they spend as an investment, they don't buy on price, they appreciate value, they can be easy to look after, whether it's because they're local or they're easy to communicate with. They're probably nice people who you like to spend time with too. There's nothing worse than dealing with a customer who you don't like as a person. You want people who are repeat customers, people who refer other people they know; they tell friends about you, they're really a fan of what you do; and also, most importantly, somebody you can add real value to.

You want to be thinking about the way you promote and attract people strategically and your attraction strategy and tactics are there to pre-sort what you do and who you do it for, to minimise your costs and improve your return on investment.

You don't want to be one of these sales or marketing people who makes one phone call and because somebody doesn't say yes, you leave them and you don't come back to them. You need to be disciplined, you need to be determined, you need to go back to people and you need to build a rapport over time.

You need to build and move people through sales stages. When it comes to actually selling or marketing, you're going to have a situation where, to start with at least, people have never heard of you. You want to move them from that position to where people say: "Who is that company? Who is that person?" Then they say, "I've heard of that person." Then you want them to say: "Yes, I know who they are." You've educated them. Then you have to get to the point where people say: "Yes, I use them," or "I buy from them." Then, finally - and this is why not just direct response but branding is really important - they see you as their only supplier of that product or service, the 'go to' person or company. When they think about what they need that you provide, you are the first person they think of; that's when you know you're being successful in a sales and marketing context.

Remember, you need to make sure that you have great sales attitudes for yourself, your company and the people you work with: you manage time correctly, you think strategically, you have a tactical approach to things, you have good or even great communication skills and you have great skills when it comes to follow-ups and presentations. You know that you have the right mindset. Your mindset is actually more important than the techniques you use, and from this comes Strategy and Entrepreneurship.

Nothing in sales, marketing or business is ever perfect; you have to understand and accept that and that's why you need the constant measurement and continual refinement, because that's why you're going to be successful. You never need to sit still and be accepting of the situation as it is at the moment; you can always decide what you want, and you can go out and get it with a level of predictability that most people in sales and marketing will just never understand, let alone deliver.

Which brings me to this point and, as in my other book, 'The Entrepreneurs Book', I ended with a quote and I want to do that again. But this time it's from a very different person, because this quote sums up so many things that this book's all about.

Obviously this book is not just about how you acquire new customers and how you adopt the ESTO approach – the Entrepreneurial, Strategic, Tactical and Operational segments – that will be an asset to your business: it's here to explain how to get things right, get what you do, how you do it, when you do it, and the ways you use and the strategies that actually work for you time and time again perfect, or as close to perfect as could ever be possible.

So I just want to finish with this quote from Mahatma Gandhi. I think it's really important that you work through this book, but equally important that you leave with this as a thought:

"Keep your thoughts positive because your thoughts become your words. Keep your words positive because your words become your behaviour. Keep your behaviour positive because your behaviour becomes your habits. Keep your habits positive because your habits become your values. Keep your values positive because your values become your destiny."

www.ingramcontent.com/pod-product-compliance
Lightning Source LLC
Chambersburg PA
CBHW071858200326
41519CB00016B/4447